What!
I have to give a speech?

What!
I have to give a speech?

Thomas J. Murphy and Kenneth Snyder

Grayson Bernard Publishers
P.O. Box 5247
Bloomington, IN 47407

Printed in the United States of America

Book design and typesetting: Addie Seabarkrob

Cover design: David J. Smith

Cover photo: Vincent Hobbs / Superstock

Library of Congress Cataloging-in-Publication Data

Murphy, Thomas, 1949 Mar. 9-
      What! I have to give a speech? / Thomas J. Murphy and Kenneth Snyder.
        p.   cm.
  ISBN 1-883790-10-7 : $12.95
  1. Public speaking—Juvenile literature. [1. Public speaking.] I. Snyder,
Kenneth, 1947- . II. Title. III. Title: I have to give a speech?
  PN4121.M79 1995
  808.5'1—dc2094-37438

                               CIP
                               AC

About the Authors

Thomas J. Murphy teaches seventh-grade English at
Greenway Middle School in Phoenix. Tom has been
promoted to the classroom after serving fifteen
years as a principal. He holds Masters' Degrees in
School Administration and Reading. Tom is co-
author of *SMART Learning: A Study Skills Guide
for Teens* and *The Skillful Learner,* a student management system. He has conducted numerous
workshops for teachers, parents, and students
throughout the country. Tom is a native of
Norristown, Pennsylvania. He and his wife, Donna,
and their two children live in Phoenix, Arizona.

Dr. Ken Snyder is a dentist and professional speaker.
For the past six years, he has traveled throughout
the United States and Canada presenting his humor
workshop, *A Chuckle a Day Keeps the Doctor
Away.* He is the founder of the Leaders of Tomorrow Foundation, Inc., a non-profit organization
dedicated to training students in communication and
leadership skills. In the past five years, his program
has been taught in over 600 classrooms throughout
Arizona. Dr. Snyder is a native of Pittsburgh,
Pennsylvania. He and his wife, JoAnn, and their
five children live in Phoenix, Arizona.

To my father, Ken, who taught me to speak up.
To my mother, Ruthie, who taught me to listen.
To my lovely wife, JoAnn, and my children, Sherri, Mike,
    Dan, Kristi, and Nancy, who are my strength and …
    to all the teachers and students who have made this
    venture a work of joy.

— K. S.

To my uncle, George Ferenz, who spoke little but
    said much.

— T. M.

Contents

Introduction

Do You Really Expect ME to Give a Speech?

Have you ever wondered what is the most common fear we all share? Here's a quick story that cuts to the heart of the matter.

> While on safari, Tom and Ken walked back to camp after a day's hunt. As they turned a bend in the path, they found themselves face to face with the biggest, most intimidating lion either one of them had ever seen. They knew that there was no time to reload their guns. Trying to outrun the lion was out of the question.
>
> Ken dropped to his knees, crying, ready to meet his maker.
>
> Tom was about to do the same, but then said, "Wait! I have an idea!" He walked up to the lion and whispered a few words.
>
> The lion looked shocked. Immediately it put its tail between its legs and ran as fast as it could into the jungle.

"Tom, it's a miracle! How did you do it? What did you say?"

Tom shrugged his shoulders and re- plied, "Simple. All I said was, 'After dinner, you will be expected to say a few words.' "

Butterflies in your stomach, stage fright, nerves, fear, terror — these are typical ways of describing what it feels like to get up before a group of people and speak (or sing or dance or play the piano). Although many people are afraid of flying, sickness, insects, or heights, the one thing that most people fear above all else is having to speak before a group. To these people, the idea of giving a speech is just as frightening as meeting a hungry lion.

Why are people so afraid of speaking in public? Can it really be that difficult or frightening?

If you think about it for a moment, you'll probably realize that the reason most people are afraid of public speaking is this: They don't know how to do it.

In this book you will find out exactly how to prepare and present a speech to a group of people, and you will discover how to overcome your fears. Even more impor- tant, you'll find out that the ability to speak in public can be valuable to you in many ways — every day.

I Don't Think I Will Ever Have to Give a Speech. (Or Will I?)

You may not think that you've ever given a speech, but you probably have. You just never thought of it that way. Suppose your family is all gathered around for Thanksgiv- ing dinner. Your dad asks you to offer a prayer of thanks- giving — that is a speech. In class or in a meeting you are asked to defend or to oppose the topic under discussion — that is a speech.

There are as many different types of speeches as there are occasions for people to gather together. Speeches might include an introduction, a thank you, an attempt to convince an audience, a humorous and entertaining presentation, an oral report in class, an interview, and a debate.

You hear people giving speeches every day. They range from a soliloquy of your favorite soap opera character to a special report on the evening news, the Mayor's talk to your class, a baseball coach honoring his team at the end-of-the-season banquet, or a pastor's Sunday sermon.

Speechmakers give more than facts about their subjects. They choose, arrange, and interpret these facts in a unique way and thus reveal their own opinions about the subject. Sometimes they reveal their own personalities and ways of looking at the world.

Now it's true that you may not have to "give a speech" every day, but the ability to organize and express your ideas can be very valuable to you — every day. If you think about it for a moment, you'll understand why.

First Impressions

What is the first thing you notice when you meet someone you have never seen before? You probably notice his or her appearance. Are they tall or short, well-dressed or shabby, attractive or not?

What is the next thing you notice about people you are meeting for the first time? It's probably the way they speak. Are they able to carry on an intelligent conversation, or do they just mumble and twitch nervously? If they don't express their ideas clearly, then you are probably going to have an unfavorable impression of them (even if their appearance is good).

The fact is that we probably make more judgments about other people based on their conversation skills than on any other single factor except their appearance. In turn, others judge us by our ability to express ourselves clearly. This is one of the most important things that affect the perception other people have of us.

As you will see on the following pages, you can learn tricks that will help you improve your ability to carry on a good conversation with your friends. Then, once you've done that, you will see how to take the next step: to learn how to give a speech before an audience.

In *Poor Richard's Almanac* Benjamin Franklin wrote, "Once you gain the reputation of being an early riser, you can get up at noon." He understood the importance of perception. The way others perceive us has a great deal to do with our identities. Franklin understood: The perception is the reality.

Your life is also affected by the way your teachers and classmates perceive you. Often without realizing it, you become very much like their expectations of you. The author Kurt Vonnegut once wrote, "Be careful who you pretend to be because pretty soon you will become that person."

In fact, there are only a few ways you can influence how others view you. If you are not a performer or an athlete, your possibilities are fairly limited. When it really comes down to it, it is your appearance and your communication skills that allow you to stand apart from the pack.

In this book we won't be able to do much about how you look or dress because that's a matter of your personal taste and finances. But we can help you improve your ability to communicate with other people. Of the four basic communication skills — speaking, writing, listening, and reading — your speaking skills have the greatest impact on how others view you.

On the following pages we will focus on those communication skills. We will show you how you can give a good impression to other people when you speak. We will also provide plenty of practice opportunities: The more you do, the better you get. One caution: "Practice doesn't make perfect; it makes permanent." So practice hard, but practice smart.

When you speak to a group of people, you have only one chance to make a good first impression. You must make the audience like you and you must give a good presentation as well. This task, like any other, is easy if you have some basic knowledge and the right tools.

The purpose of this book is to provide you with a manual of basic communication skills. Communication is an essential part of self-esteem and is one of the most important skills an individual can possess. Mastery of communication skills not only contributes to greater self-confidence; it also shines a spotlight on your positive qualities for others to see.

Skyscrapers and bridges are not built in a day or a week; they are constructed over long periods of time, and they require a master plan, craftsmanship, and especially patience. We will provide the master plan and the tools you will need to communicate effectively and to present yourself in a positive light. You must provide the time, the effort, and especially the patience to master the craft so that you can communicate convincingly with others, whether it's with a group of friends at school or with an audience waiting to hear what you have to say.

What Does a Good Speech Look Like (and Sound Like)?

As a beginning speaker you need to understand that there are two separate processes you must go through — building the content of the speech itself and learning how to present it. At first, keep it simple and limit your speech to something you already know about. Here are four suggestions:

1. Give a speech that teaches the audience something you know how to do.
2. Take something complex and simplify it.
3. Take a stand on an issue you care about.
4. Tell about an unusual experience you have had.

Let's look at a good speech so that you can see what you will be working toward. Fifth-grader Jessica decided to talk about ventriloquism — a subject she knew a great deal about. By following the guidelines we will give on the following pages, you can give a speech just as good as this one.

> (Jessica holds a Lambchop© puppet in her left hand. The puppet's mouth moves as if speaking. Jessica speaks in a funny voice.)
>
> Wouldn't you like to learn to talk just like me? Well, now you can because my friend Jessica is going to teach you to become a ven-trill-o-kissed.
>
> (Jessica speaks) No, no, Baby Lambchops, that's a ventriloquist.
>
> (Baby Lambchops replies) Sorrrry.
>
> (Jessica says in a kind tone) That's O.K.

(Jessica sets the puppet down.)

A ventriloquist is a person who makes puppets come to life through voices. Ventriloquism isn't just fun; you can use it to entertain groups of people, or you can even make it your occupation when you get older.

The first thing you need to know about ventriloquism is how to get started. You could take a class if one is available. If not, you might go to the library and find a book on ventriloquism. I recommend *Magic With Your Voice* by George Schindler because it has a lot of good tips. A book on ventriloquism will tell you about different techniques you can use.

One technique is the breathing technique. It's very important because when you change voices you have to learn to breathe very quickly. The book will also show you how to practice without moving your mouth.

First you have to practice the vowels *a, e, i, o, u.* All you do is put your teeth together like this (Jessica purses her lips and clenches her teeth) and speak in a normal voice, *a — e — i — o — u.* It's very simple. (Jessica points to a prop, the letters, on the board, as she pronounces each letter.) Letters like *w, b, f, v,* and *m* are more difficult to say without moving your mouth and they require a lot more practice.

The next thing I want to talk to you about is puppets. Puppets range from soft puppets to stuffed puppets all the way to wooden puppets. The main thing is that you need to get one with a movable mouth.

The next thing I want to talk about is voices. Before you begin to develop the voice, you should buy the puppet. You want to be sure that the voice fits the puppet's character. For example, you wouldn't want to put a Robin Leach voice with a cowboy puppet. That just wouldn't work out very well.

Once you have your puppet and a special voice, practice in front of the mirror. Don't worry at first about not moving your mouth. Here's a good tip: move the puppet's mouth for every syllable you say. For example (Jessica picks up large lion puppet and in a roaring voices says while moving the lion's mouth with each new syllable) *a — e — i — o — u- - i —am — the — li — on.* Gradually, if you practice enough you'll be able to do the puppet's voice without moving your mouth. By then you become a ventriloquist.

Here's a quick summary of what I just said. Go to the library and take out a book on ventriloquism. Then get a puppet, create a voice, and practice, practice, practice.

Ventriloquism has a lot of good uses, but I think one of the best is that you get to meet a lot of unusual — but lovable — friends (Jessica shows a small little old lady sock puppet on her hand) like my friend Sadie here.

(Sadie says) That's right Jessica. I'm your frieeeeenddd for life.

(Jessica shrugs and says) See what I mean?

I hope you'll try ventriloquism today. ■

Part One

Getting Ready

In many ways, understanding how to present a speech is like sighting an iceberg for the first time. The parts you can see represent only 10% of the whole iceberg. The rest is hidden under the surface. Before you ever say a word to an audience, there's a lot of behind-the-scenes preparation to do. You must choose a topic, gather information, and organize your ideas in an interesting way that makes sense to you. Only then can you think about presenting these ideas in a speech that holds the audience's attention.

Chapter

1

Is Giving a Speech Anything Like Talking?

Suppose your social studies teacher came up to you and said, "I'd like you to give a short report to the class next Monday. Be prepared to speak for five minutes on a topic we've been studying that really interests you."

After you manage to stop shaking with fright you might say, "What? ME, give a speech? But I don't know HOW!"

This is the way most of us would react if we were asked to speak to a group. Even if we knew the people we were speaking to, we would still feel that we weren't sure how to stand up in front of them and deliver a speech.

You may not be asked to stand up and deliver a speech to an audience every day, but there is one thing you probably do every day: Talk to other people. You engage in conversation with them, and you do this so often that you probably don't even notice that you often have to organize your thoughts and ideas so you can express them clearly to others. In a way, that's what a speech is: an organized presentation of your thoughts and ideas.

But, you say, "Talking to my friends and family is not like making a speech. I already know them, and we're just talking." It's true that you do know your family and friends, but even when you are "just talking" to them you do something that can be a great help when you speak to a larger group of people.

The Difference between Talking and Saying Something

When you're having a conversation about something that is important, you try to convince other people that you know what you are talking about. You try to convince them that your opinions are worthwhile because you can back them up with good, solid information. If you rely on facts that others can check for themselves, then they realize that you really do know what you're talking about. You also want to make the conversation — and thus yourself — interesting. If you can do this, you're not just talking — you're actually saying something.

Compare the following conversations. In each of them, two people are discussing a movie they just saw:

First Conversation:
"Did you see *In the Name of the Father?*"
"Yeah. It was great."
"Yeah. Lots of good stuff in it."
"Yeah. It was cool."
"Yeah. I liked it a lot."
"Yeah. Me too."

Second Conversation:
"What did you think of *In the Name of the Father?*"

"Well, I think it is the greatest Irish story since the one with Tom Cruise and Nicole Kidman."

"Do you mean *Far and Away?* Well, I agree. I thought the acting was terrific."

"Yes. The girl's father was really convincing."

"But I thought the ending was better. I kept looking at my watch. I knew the movie was close to over, but I wanted it to just keep going."

"The last scene even made my boyfriend cry. I looked over to see his reaction and he brushed the tears from his cheek."

"You're kidding, Mr. Cool Hand Luke himself? I'd give a million dollars to have seen that."

"What an excellent movie. I think it'll win the Oscar. I definitely want to see it again."

What is the difference between these two conversations? In the first, we hear only that the movie was "great" and "cool" and "I liked it." This is all right as an expression of personal preference, but it doesn't tell us much about why the movie was enjoyable. It's just small-talk.

In the second conversation we get a much better idea of why the two girls thought the movie was good. Each person actually gives specific reasons for her opinions. Others can judge these things for themselves. They do not have to agree, but at least they know what they are talking about, and they have something to say.

With a little thought, you can do more than just say that you liked this or didn't like that; you can say why you thought a certain movie or TV show was good (or bad).

If you can talk to your friends in an interesting way, then you can organize your thoughts so that you feel confident about speaking before a larger group. This doesn't have to be scary — if you've prepared yourself by deciding what you want to say and how you want to say it. We're going to start showing you how this can be done by looking at the very thing we've just been talking about: everyday conversations.

The Basics of Everyday Conversation

When you are talking with your friends and family, do you ever notice that there are several different kinds of conversations? Sometimes you may just shoot the breeze with your friends. Sometimes you may argue about something with your brothers and sisters. Other times you may engage in a serious discussion about a subject that is important to you. In a conversation, you may just react to what others say ("Yeah, I like that, too") or you may bring up an idea that you've thought about and that is important to you.

No matter what situation you encounter, you will be able to talk more convincingly and feel more confident if you remember **The Five Golden Rules Of Conversation.**

Rule 1: Create Interest

One of the questions that students ask most often is, "How do I keep a conversation going?" This is a situation you will probably encounter on a date, hanging out with friends, meeting new people, and especially with parents. We all find ourselves in this uncomfortable position from time to time. Usually there is an awkward silence or the conversation deteriorates into meaningless drivel.

> You can help to keep a conversation going by asking open-ended questions that require more than just a *Yes* or *No* answer. Open-ended questions create interest and encourage the answerer to participate in the conversation.

Don't ask: "Are you looking forward to going to high school"?

Instead, say: "What are you especially looking forward to in high school?" or "What frightens you when you think about high school?"

Don't ask: "Did you see *Schindler's List?*"

Instead, say: "What's the best movie you've seen recently? Why do you think so?"

Don't ask: "Do you play football?"

Instead, say: "What school activities do you prefer? Why? What school activities do you avoid? Why?"

Rule 2: Avoid the *"I"* Disease

If you want to give yourself a shock, tape-record one of your conversations or review one of your notes or letters to a friend. Notice how many times you used the word *I*, especially at the beginning of sentences:

> *I* did this.
> *I* did that.
> *I* am this.
> *I* am that.
> *I* think . . .
> *I* believe . . .
> *I* like . . .
> *I, YI, YI, YI, YI . . .*

You do not impress people if you are not able to talk about anything except yourself and your experiences. By hogging the conversation with *"I"* messages, you soon become B-O-R-I-N-G.

> Once a young gentleman tried to impress his date by bragging about himself. After about half an hour he decided it was her turn to talk.
> "That's enough talk about me," he said.
> "Tell me, what do you think about me?"

Unless you want people to avoid you as if you have bad breath, avoid the disease.

> There is no word in the English language smaller than the word *I*. Don't let it be the largest word in your vocabulary.

Rule 3: Don't Interrupt

This rule speaks for itself. When you talk to someone else, he or she may say something that instantly brings an idea to your mind. Even though you're eager to say what you're thinking, wait your turn to share your ideas. Don't interrupt other people when they are talking (just as you would not want to be interrupted when you are talking).

> The road to good conversation is a two-way street. Nobody wants to travel a road filled with potholes and detours. ***Don't Interrupt.***

Rule 4: Don't Gossip

Surely your mom told you, "If you can't say something nice about a person, don't say anything."

Another version is, "A wise man (or woman) once said — nothing!"

This is simple and true — and also profound. Sometimes people spread dirt about others because they think it will make them look superior. This is never the case. If you don't show respect for others, then others will lose respect for you.

Remember: when you throw dirt on others, your hands get dirty. If someone is telling you the latest rumors, then you can be sure they are telling others about you.

If you find yourself in a conversation involving gossip, there's an easy way to deal with the problem: just casually switch to another topic.

There are so many wonderful, interesting things to talk about; why waste your time and energy on something that has absolutely no benefit — gossip?

Rule 5: Listen. Then listen harder.

It is no accident that God made us with two eyes, two ears, and only one mouth. This is a simple 2-to-1 proportion that we must keep in mind. Humans seem to fare much better when they watch and listen twice as much as they speak. And when they do speak, they should make it worthwhile.

People love good listeners; they are often among the most sought-after friends. Usually, when a problem develops among friends or with parents, it is because of poor listening. Common phrases that we hear are:

"Mom, you never listen to me!"
"Son, you just don't listen!"

Fifty percent of communication is good listening.

This means not only listening with our ears but with our minds, with our senses, and especially with our hearts. Good listening brings information to the listener and inspiration to the speaker. All too often, as someone is speaking we are busy rushing ahead in our minds to what we are going to say next. Successful people are excellent listeners. They already know their own thoughts. They want to gather additional information by listening to the thoughts of others.

❖ Wrapping It Up:
What Did You Learn in This Chapter?

In this chapter we showed you how to carry on a good conversation by obeying **The Five Golden Rules.**

- Create interest by asking open-ended questions.
- Avoid the *"I"* disease.
- Don't interrupt.
- Don't gossip.
- Listen!

These rules are simple and easy to master. With a little effort, you can become an exceptional conversationalist — and popular, too.

❖ Now Try This:
Applying What You Have Learned

1. Listen to the conversations of other people and evaluate them. How effectively were the five rules used in the conversation? What was the result?

2. Carry on conversations with parents, friends, or neighbors.

As you are talking, practice using the Five Golden Rules of Conversation. In particular, try to create interest by asking open-ended questions, and try to avoid the *"I"* disease.

3. Study other people when they speak, whether they are engaged in a conversation or are giving a speech. How often do they slip into some of the attention-losers that were listed at the end of this chapter?

How often do you talk too fast or too slow or fail to speak clearly? What changes do you need to make in order to improve your communication skills?

Chapter
2

What Should I Talk About?

Picking a Topic and Finding Information

The assignment to give a speech causes problems for most students. They lack the know-how to plan and deliver a speech. They don't know how to get information on a topic so that they can talk about it. And perhaps the biggest problem of all is that they lack the confidence in themselves to believe they have something worth saying to an audience.

Too many times, students end up at the last minute plagiarizing — copying information that someone else has written — and passing it off as their own. This is not only dishonest; it also means that the student has not learned anything, because copying is not learning. However, you can have something worthwhile to say and you can learn how to say it effectively.

Suppose your assignment is to give a speech on castles as part of a social studies unit on the Middle Ages. What would you do? Since you have probably never seen a real castle, you may feel that you are at a disadvantage. In order to give this speech, you are going to have to learn a lot about castles.

Whether you're exploring a topic in chemistry, math, baseball, or castles, you must go through a similar learning process:

- First, you must gather new information. In order to do this you must understand what useful information is, where to find it, how to use it, and how to get rid of information that doesn't fit your goals.
- Then, you must organize and make sense of that information. You must construct your own meaning, a personal message that makes sense to you because of what you've learned.
- Finally, you must be able to use the information in a creative way. You must be able to express it clearly so that others can understand it.

When you finally get to demonstrate what you've learned, it's called application — the part of the learning process that belongs to you. It is the time when you show ownership of what you've learned. This is the demonstration phase when you let others know what you know by giving a speech, writing a report, or even answering a question in class. But the real payoff is in the real world when your speech brings in twenty new customers, your report gets you a promotion, or your answer to one question helps you get your dream job.

Selecting a Topic

Once you have been asked to make a speech, the first task (and sometimes the hardest) is what your speech will be about — the topic. Here are two pieces of advice: If the teacher gives you the opportunity, by all means *pick a topic that interests you.* If you are not interested in your topic, you can be pretty sure that your audience won't be, either. On the other hand, if you select a topic that you are truly interested in, then your enthusiasm will spill over to the audience. You will be able to direct more energy to your presentation and, as a result, find more interesting and creative ways to present your material. This in itself will create audience interest.

Pick a topic that you know something about. This doesn't mean you have to know more than everyone in the audience about the topic, but you should at least be familiar with your topic. No professional speaker would get up in front of an audience and speak on a topic that was totally unfamiliar. You shouldn't, either. For a beginning speaker there will be enough nervousness just facing an audience. You don't want to compound that nervousness by trying to remember information you don't really know.

Sometimes students are frustrated when their teachers assign them topics. For example, let's say that you've been assigned to speak on the culture of Japan. You may not know much about Japan other than that your family car is a Toyota. When you're in a situation like this, make the most of it — or, to put it another way, when life hands you lemons, make lemonade. In such a case, focus on that part of the culture that interests you the most. If you like martial arts, speak on judo; if you like plants, speak on bonsai; if you like to eat, you could talk about sashimi and sushi.

Some people become paralyzed at the thought of picking a topic. Perhaps they lack the self-confidence to believe that they really know anything worth saying. Others are foggy about topics they really do know and could share with others. Still others are put off at the thought of the long process that awaits them. Keep it simple. Do one step at a time. Now is the time to pick a topic — so make it one that interests you.

Here is a menu of possible topics. It may inspire you to think of related topics.

Tell About Unusual Experiences

stage fright, moving, a big mistake, a re-union, getting lost in a foreign country, getting hurt, getting caught, cleaning up, being a friend, flirting.

Describe Unusual

People: My Dad (An Easter Seal Poster Boy), grandma in the Peace Corps, coach, neighbor, bus driver, someone you spend time with in the summer, someone you wish you were like, someone who bugs you, your rival, first crush, meeting a celebrity, or the death of a classmate

Places: Space Camp, visiting a foreign country, Yellowstone Park, what to do in Las Vegas when you're too young to gamble, a local hangout, hiding place, attic, rooftop, alley, beach, barn, river, canyon, zoo, yard, corner

Things: movie, poster, old sea chest, gilded mirror, book, video game, model, mountain bike, in-line skates

Teach the Audience How to . . .

baby-sit, use ventriloquism, practice good nutrition, do a term paper on a Macintosh, mountain bike, deal with stress, fly cast… decorate your room, mime, read music, eat

spaghetti, make a team, improve your
memory, care for a pet... entertain, impress
your teacher, earn extra money... throw a
party, get in shape, climb a mountain ...
take a picture, windsurf

Simplify a Complicated Idea

American Sign Language, how an internal
combustion engine works, genetics, how an
airplane stays in the air, what is a root
canal, arthroscopic surgery, how rust occurs, magic, how to explain dreams

Causes of:

War in Bosnia, acid rain, tooth decay, acne,
hiccups, fights, tornadoes, floods, shin
splints, dropouts, failing a class, cheating

Definition of:

class, generation gap, success, popularity, a
good time, to hassle, radical, conservative,
soul, grandma, nerd, loyalty, astrology,
Kosher, algebra

Take a Stand on an Idea You Care About

animal experimentation, teen curfews, crash
diets, hot political topics, eliminating smok-
ing in public places, sports salaries, censorship, an unfair school rule, making airbags
mandatory, year-round school, hunting, truth
in advertising, discrimination against

Narrow the Topic

Think carefully about the information you will gather
before you go chasing your tail. Suppose you choose the
topic baseball. As you begin your research you will discover how unwieldy this broad topic is. You might find you
would be better off zeroing in on one of the following:

How baseball has changed in the last
   ten years
The superstars of the Negro League
Are baseball salaries too high?
The fundamentals of hitting
Baseball's confusing rules, and much,
   much more.

Where to Begin

Before you can speak about a topic, you must find out as much about it as you can. You'll be surprised to discover how much information is readily available on almost any topic you can think of (including castles). You can look in libraries, magazines, and museums, of course, but sometimes your most important source of information turns out to be other people who are experts on the topic. They might be right at hand.

Plan your gathering steps or you will lose valuable time and become frustrated before you even begin. Before you go to the library, only to discover that you don't know what to look for, think of the people you might first talk to about this subject.

The yellow pages of the phone book are loaded with experts on practically any topic under the sun. These people can give you valuable information in a short time, and you don't even have to leave your house. These experts also can direct you to where you must go next in your search. Interviews are the easiest way to start.

Speech Based on Two Interviews

Seventh-grader Vanessa gave this well-informed speech based on two interviews with her pediatrician. The first was preliminary and done by telephone. Making the presentation, Vanessa is dressed in green operating room scrubs, with a surgical mask around her neck for effect.

The Pediatric Zone

Hi, I'm Vanessa Bragg, M.D. This is my patient, Emily Schazen (holds up a life-sized infant doll).

Who here would like to be a doctor when you grow up? Did you know that to be a doctor takes twenty-five years of schooling if you count elementary school, high school, college, medical school, internships, and residencies? As if that wasn't enough, you must maintain an A average to even get into medical school. And after graduation a doctor still has to attend medical workshops and keep up on the latest information by reading medical journals (displays a medical journal).

I'm a pediatrician, a doctor who takes care of newborns to children 17 and 18 years of age. I treat many sicknessess, diseases, viruses, and colds. I even take care of well children. This is called preventative medicine.

People often ask me how I know which medicine to use or which sickness it is. In order to find out, I follow some basic steps. First I take a medical history on each of my patients. Then I give the patient a physical exam. I must be able to read their signs and symptoms to know which disease the patient might have. Then I prescribe the

necessary treatment or medicine to cure the
disease.

I see patients who need checkups, kids
with mild illnesses, and well children. Sometimes I am called to the hospital when a
baby is born if the obstetrician suspects the
baby is going to be ill when it is born.

I became a doctor because I love
children. I love taking care of them and
making them feel better. I love to see the
twinkle in their eye and the smile on their
face when they're no longer ill.

I'm going to explain some of the medical
instruments and medicines I use. I'm also
going to tell you about five different tests
which are part of the Apgar scale.

I must use many different types of
medicines. Some are over-the-counter
drugs, which means that they can be bought
from any pharmacy without a doctor's
prescription (holds up Pediacare, a decon-
gestant). Here's an antibiotic (holds up
prescription drug). This may be adminis-
tered by capsule or injection. And here's the
much-feared needle that allows the serum
to get into the baby's system. When babies
can't swallow a capsule they must get an
injection. See, this isn't so scary, is it?

I also have many instruments. (Displays
the stethoscope.) The stethoscope allows
me to listen to the heart and to check a
patient's breathing. (Displays the blood-
pressure cuff.) Here's a blood-pressure cuff,

which goes around your arm and allows me to check your blood pressure. (Displays a Petri dish.) This is a Petri dish which is used to grow germs in a laboratory. As you can see, there is something growing on this one. If a patient has a sore throat, I will take this cotton swab and rub the throat. I transfer what's on the swab into the Petri dish. If germs grow we'll know you have an infection and we'll be able to identify which germ we must treat.

I give many medical tests, too. One is the Apgar. This test was developed in the early 1940s by Virginia Apgar to help determine the health of a baby when it is born. Doctors are taught to ask themselves two questions: How is the baby doing now? How will the baby be in the next two weeks?

To determine this I must give the baby five simple tests. I will demonstrate this now on my patient Emily. (She puts on surgical gloves, claps her hands, and picks up the doll.) I'm going to check Emily's Apgar score (shows the Apgar chart). The five tests involve heart rate, muscle tone, color, respiratory effects, and reflexes.

To determine the heart rate I use the stethoscope. (She demonstrates on Emily, then turns to her chart and with a black marker checks the appropriate score for Emily.) Apgar scores range from zero to two, with two being the best. Emily receives a two for this category — heart rate. Less than 60 is scored a zero; 60-100 is one; and above one hundred is two. Emily received a two because her heart rate was 105. I will record her score and make a note of the heart rate on her medical chart. (She writes the score into a manila folder.)

Next we will check muscle tone to see how limp or strong Emily's muscles are. (She holds the infant and bends her at all joints.) Emily is not unusually limp, nor is she very strong. On this test she scores a one. (Records score on chart and in medical folder.)

Now we will check Emily's color. Here, babies get zero if they are blue, one if their hands and feet are pink, and two if the whole baby is pink. Since Emily is very pink, I give her a two on color. (She records the score on the Apgar chart and in medical folder.)

Next I'll take my trusty little hammer and check Emily's reflexes. (She gently taps Emily on both knees and demonstrates reflex movement.) As you can see, Emily has very good reflexes. She gets a two.

Finally, I'll check her respiratory effect by placing the stethoscope first on her chest and then on her back while listening carefully to her lungs. Her lungs sound clear and she is breathing normally. Again, she receives a two. If she got a zero on that she would be dead. (Records score on chart and in medical folder.)

Now let's add up Emily's score and see how healthy she is. She scores a nine out of ten, which is very healthy.

There are many fields an aspiring doctor may pursue: plastic surgery, therapy, general practice, internal medicine, cardiology, and my particular favorite, the pediatric zone.

If you're having a hard time deciding what you want to be when you grow up, perhaps you'll think back to my speech and maybe you too can see yourself as a doctor. By the way, I personally stay away from giving the shots because that's my nurse's job.

Learning to Gather Information

Let's play a little game. It will be more fun and will work better if you can find a partner; see if you can get an adult to join in. This game is a "warm-up" for research. The idea of the game is to figure out how to gather information about the items below. You do not have to actually gather it. Instead, spend your time thinking of how and where you could locate each item in the fastest and easiest manner possible.

Brainstorm ways to find this information. Remember: Your objective is to come up with the correct information in the shortest amount of time and with the least amount of effort.

See who is the most clever sleuth. Not only will you learn a variety of new places to seek information; you will also be certain that two heads are better than one. Your opponents or partner will teach you a lot about solving the mysteries of research.

Before you act, consider your options. Which is the fastest, cheapest, most valuable to your report? You may not have access to all of them, depending on where you live, so make the most of what information you can acquire locally.

1. A rattlesnake skin.
2. A label from a product made in a city with a population between 150,000 and 500,000.
3. A commemorative stamp.
4. A postcard from an eighteenth-century landmark.
5. The name of the first African-American to be named Poet Laureate of America.
6. The title, author, and year of publication of the first written complete history of your state.
7. The President's birth date.
8. A map of the city streets in your state's largest city.

Let's review the places where you might easily track down each of the items above:

1. Did you try a telephone book? Look up shoes or boots. Is there a boot factory in your town? How about a zoo? Do you know what a herpetologist is ?

2. Did you start in your cupboard by checking some possible companies? Did you think of an almanac or an atlas? A dictionary is also a good starting place. Find a list of towns that fit the population criteria. Now try to make some connections. Are there any obvious companies from that town?

3. A call to the Post Office might be in order here. They sell stamps and might have what you want. They might also be able to tell you about local stamp collectors. Or try looking up stamps, philatelic, or antiquarian shops in the yellow pages. Your local hobby shops are a place to start.

4. This is the toughest one. The yellow pages won't have historical societies listed as a guide word but you can look under Museums or Tourist Attractions. The first thing you need to know is that the 18th century means between 1700-1799. Since America was not really a nation until the last quarter of the century, you need to think about Spanish missions, French trading posts, and British settlements. Philadelphia, Boston, and New York all have many historical landmarks that fit this criterion. You could fax or call (if your parents don't mind) or have someone send a postcard.

5. This one's easy. If you have CD Newsbank at your school or local library, type in the key words POET LAUREATE and you will see that Rita Dove Brown was granted that honor.

6. Remember: The yellow pages won't list historical societies, so look under Museums or Tourist Attractions. Every state has at least one historical society that maintains a library, usually located in the biggest city or your state capital. One telephone call to the reference librarian will answer your question. Have your pencil and paper ready.

7. Again, this is a pretty simple one. There are three or four places you might look for this one. The first is the newest almanac, the second is *Who's Who in America,* and the third is the blue pages — they are a place for government telephone numbers. Look up federal government, not local, — then General Services Administration 1-800-359-3997. They will put you on track. The last place you might check is the local party headquarters (provided you know which party the President belongs to). An easy way out is to call the reference librarian at your local library. You should keep that phone number handy.

8. Your local AAA (Automobile Association of America), a travel agent, or your trusty local library will have the answer to this one.

We hope that the scavenger hunt made its point: Information is all around you. And by far, people are the best sources of information. Plan to include other people as you begin gathering information about a topic. Combine people power with the telephone or even a modem and you have unlimited capacity to gather data without leaving your room. Your first stop when researching a topic ought to be a brainstorming session with some study partners. Have a phone book handy and the phone number of the reference librarian.

After you've looked for creative ways to find out about castles without leaving home, your next stop should be the children's section of the library. Here the materials are written in simple terms, with a lot of color and graphics. But don't be fooled! Even if you're not a "little kid," you can still find much valuable information that can set you on the right track. Because these books usually focus on only the most important points, they can help you organize your speech or oral report by identifying these important points right away. Then you can set out to find more information and to add details that you will find in books for "big kids."

Don't spend a lot of time here. Check the card catalogue, find the call numbers, go to the appropriate section, and take the books on castles to the closest table. Spend no more than ten minutes looking through them, and then take the best with you for closer reading

As you read the books, fill your head with information. As you start to understand some things about castles, you will discover you already know more than you thought. Add important new information you have found to your notes.

Before you begin your "real" research, think of your topic in terms of a problem to solve. That question may lead to another that's related. Good; you're narrowing the topic. Then you don't just say, "I've got to give a report on baseball" and throw in everything you can find about the national pastime. Instead, you begin to formulate some questions as you get more information. Finally, you focus on a question that can yield a specific topic for your report: "How did they do this?" or "Why did they do that?" or "When did this happen?"

When you read about baseball played in 1920's, you might wonder why there were only white players in the major leagues. You might notice the emergence of the commissioner's role after the Black Sox scandal in the 1919 World Series. You might even trace the development of the first genuine American sports hero, Babe Ruth, and thus the birth of the superstar.

When you research castles, which were built before the invention of electricity and power machinery, you will think of obvious problems that had to be solved by those who built them: "How did they keep these huge stone buildings from falling down?" or "How did they get all those heavy stones to the top of the castle?" If you are having difficulty trying to find a problem to provide the focus for your report, try brainstorming with study pals. Discuss castles with someone who knows about them, or view a videotape like *Castles* by David McCauley.

Once you have a problem to focus on, you're ready for some real research.

Always think technology first: Use the electronic media and CD ROM, which allow you to gather information with a touch of your finger. The CD ROM can also show you pictures and play audio tapes. It is a fast and accurate way to gather data.

Next, see if there are key words that would give you information, too. The librarian can become your greatest ally at this point. As you read about castles, you will encounter words such as *Renaissance, fortress,* and *medieval.* Find out more about these words; they may help you uncover some hidden information.

While you're searching, you should be revising your problem. Because you did not know much about castles when you began, there will probably be surprises in your research that may change your focus. At about this time in the gathering process, patience becomes an important factor. Don't be frustrated. Just read on and keep filling your head with information.

Record Information as You Find It

Gathering information is a lot like holding an icicle: you know you've got it while it's there, but when it melts away, it's gone. Facts from your research are lost without some means of recording them. Your notes are your deep-freeze, your record. Whenever you find new information, write it down. But be sure you don't clutter up your notebook with too much trivial stuff. The way you make notes is important.

Active learners don't just copy words: They make notes because they read and listen and think before they write. Note-makers are decision makers. They are disciplined: They select a helpful method of taking notes and they write only the important, useful information. Students tend to rely too much on encyclopedias. Encyclopedia articles contain information from many sources. These articles are carefully summarized. As you prepare your speech, this information may appear attractive — but ask yourself, do I really I understand this? If not, look further.

Sharon was assigned a speech in science class. Her topic had to have something to do with genetics. She chose the topic *twins* because a set of twins lived next door. Sharon thought they might become a good source for her research. Before she talked to them, she decided to go to the local public library and was able to find the following information in *Compton's Encyclopedia:*

Twins

A woman normally releases a single egg from an ovary about once a month. Once the egg is fertilized by a sperm cell, it is called a zygote. It is then implanted in the wall of the uterus where it develops until birth. (see also Embryology; Reproductive System.)

Occasionally two or more eggs are released. In this case, each egg can be fertilized by a different sperm cell. Two separate fertilized eggs produce fraternal (also called dizygotic, or two-egg) twins. Identical (monozygotic, or one-egg) twins result when a single zygote divides in two and develops as two separate embryos. Why this division of the zygote occurs is unknown. Other multiple births can result from the simultaneous occurrence of both events, so that among triplets, two may be identical and the third fraternal.

Although some fraternal twins look very similar, they are no more alike than siblings (brothers or sisters) born years apart. They may be the same or different sexes. Identical twins, on the other hand, are formed from the same genetic material and are always the same in sex, blood type, biochemical detail, and appearance. (see also Genetics.) Their fingerprints are slightly different, however, and one twin is usually more dominant or outgoing in personality.

Just as with some siblings born at different times, fraternal twins sometimes look remarkably alike, so that appearance alone is no certain indication that twins are identical. Fraternal twins can often be recognized at birth if there are two separate placentas (also called afterbirths), because identical twins always share a single placenta. Since the two placentas of fraternal twins can fuse together, however, the presence of a single placenta is no guarantee that twins are identical. The only certain diagnosis is genetic analysis.

Studies of identical twins who were raised apart are providing data that seem to indicate that heredity may influence traits once assumed to be environmentally determined. Some twins have almost identical health problems, such as cyclic headaches, high blood pressure, and even infections. Intelligence quotients (IQ), brain wave patterns, personalities, handwriting, and even hobbies can also be amazingly similar.

There are currently an estimated 2 million sets of twins…

Next she went to the juvenile section to see if there was any less-technical information that would be easier to understand. Here she found an excellent book, *Amazing Investigations: Twins* by Jay Ingram, 90 pages covering a variety of twin issues. It was colorful and fun to read. Look at her notes below. Notice how much easier some ideas and notes are to work with.

Famous twins

Dear Ann(Landers) and Dear Abby (van Buren)- born Pauline Esther and Esther Pauline Friedman In school did everything the same, dress, activities, etc.- friends called them Kate and Duplicate- never separated until marriage-double ceremony. Now- write columns for rival newspapers.

Chang and Eng- born Thailand -1811, moved to US., joined circus, married sisters- had 22 kids 1811 Thailand was called Siam. Had separate homes, spent 3 days in one-three days in other. Died 1874 within 3 hrs. of each other

Romulus and Remus-founders of Rome

Gemini- constellation, astro. sign

Siamese twins

identical twins- start as one egg embryo splits in two- each develops

twins usually a little smaller than other children (<6 lbs. vs >7 lbs.)

usually born a few wks. earlier

identical twins = 1/300 births

identical twins, est. 50 million pairs in world

split early = true identical twins

split later = mirror image twins
split late = Siamese twins- some can be
    separated, some no(vital organs)
identical twins = exact same sets of genes
fingerprints are close-not exactly alike
one twin is born 1st.- second is usually born
    few min. later, record is 147 days later
mothers of twins are more likely to have
    more e.g. Mrs. M. L. Pearson of FL 7
    sets of twins
telepathy- one sister feels labor pains while
    twin is having a baby e.g. twin feels
    sharp chest pains while brother has
    heart operation.

Organizing: Making Sense of Information

You've gathered the information and you've got it safely tucked away in your notes. Now all that's left is writing it out on note cards, right? WRONG!

Writing out what you've gathered is not the same as understanding it. In other words, you must fit individual bits of information into a pattern that shows the overall picture. You see how things relate to one another. You can even develop new patterns with what you know. You organize the material in order to understand it.

When students know little or nothing about the topic, they tend to want to copy large pieces of data without trying to understand how they fit together. Don't be fooled; your teacher and your audience already recognize your dilemma. Remember: The purpose for the speech is to get you to build your knowledge base. Students who do their one-stop shopping in the *World Book* give themselves away because their finished product is too tightly organized and too smooth for what they know.

The real trap is that you cannot use all the information you've gathered and recorded. You will have to discard some of the information that doesn't fit the topic you are developing.

Students are lazy or sometimes manage their time poorly by waiting to the last minute. They refuse to accept responsibility for their assignment and are looking for the easiest way out. One of the greatest temptations in the world is the idea of copying someone else's words.
It doesn't work.

Returning to Sharon, after she had gathered her information, it was time to group similar bits of information to see what main headings might be developed.

FAMOUS TWINS
Ann Landers and Abby Van Buren
identical twins
born Pauline Esther and Esther Pauline
    Friedman
so much alike their friends called them Kate
    and Duplicate
always together until wedding day- double
    ceremony
write for rival newspapers- Dear Ann and
    Dear Abby
Romulus and Remus, mythical founders of
    Rome
Gemini- constellation, astrological sign

INTERESTING FACTS ABOUT TWINS
identical twins have exact same set of
    genes
fingerprints of identical twins are close but
    not exactly alike

one twin is born first, the other usually a few
   minutes later
record is 147 days later
mothers of twins are more likely to have
   twins again
Mrs. M. L. Pearson of Florida has had seven
   sets of twins

HOW TWINS FORM
identical twins start as one egg, embryo
   splits in two, each develops
usually a little smaller than other babies,
   (<6 lbs. vs >7 lbs.)
usually born a few weeks earlier than most
   babies
chance of identical twins is 1/300
estimated that there are 30 million sets of
   identical twins in the world
egg splits early = identical twins
egg splits later = mirror image twins
egg splits real late = Siamese twins

identical twins - one egg splits
fraternal twins - two eggs develop at same
   time
Siamese twins - identical twins that don't
   completely split

SIAMESE TWINS
identical twins where egg splits very late
   and thus incompletely today can be
   separated if joined only by muscle, bone
   cartilage or tissue
cannot be separated if vital organs are
   shared

sometimes are separated with one dying so
    other can live a normal life
Chang and Eng
moved to US. and joined circus
born in Thailand in 1811,
married sisters
had 22 kids
kept separate homes, spent 3 days in one
    then 3 days in the other
in 1811 Thailand was called Siam
died in 1874 within 3 hrs. of each other

INTERVIEW WITH NEIGHBORS
Dan and Dave Rice 10 yrs. old identical
have twins cousins
switch class story
Dan felt Dave's pain story
what they like - friendship, attention
what they don't like - lack of identity, people
    getting them mixed up, attention

OTHER INFORMATION
twice as many fraternal twins as identical
most animals have multiple births
also triplets, quadruplets, and quintuplets-
    called super twins
Jim Lewis and Jim Springer- separated at 4
    weeks, met again 39 yrs. later
twins and mental telepathy

Retrieve Information

Your brain can hold as many as ten million volumes of
information. That's a lot of books. The trick is knowing
how to pull out the bits you need when you need them, just

as you do with the card catalog in the library (whether it's computerized or index cards). We will teach you a reliable organization technique that allows you to retrieve and use information when you need it. It's called the S-MAP, or the Speaker's Master Action Plan.

Using What You Find

The final product, the speech, is the time to show that you really do know something about your topic. You are applying what you have learned. You will learn to do this in the next chapters.

❖ Wrapping It Up:
What Did You Learn in This Chapter?

The Learning Process

At the beginning of this chapter we talked about the learning process that each of us goes through when we first encounter a new subject. First we must receive information about the subject; then we must sense that information; and finally we must understand it so well that we can — what we know to other people. Can you think of a topic on which you have gone through this learning process?

Pick a Topic

When you think about a subject for your report or speech, it is important to find a topic that is not too broad or vague. You can't cover the history of the world in a ten-minute speech, but you can give an interesting report telling what happened at the villages of Concord and Lexington in Massachusetts on the first day of the Revolutionary War.

Also approach your topic as a problem to be solved. This will help to focus your research because you won't just be copying down information at random; you will be looking for the answers to questions such as "How did they do that?" or "When did this happen?"

Organize to Understand New Information

Organize your search for information because it gets you to think about what you already know, suggests questions that you can try to answer, and directs you toward new information that will broaden your understanding of the subject.

❖ Now Try This:
Applying What You Have Learned

1. Choose five broad topics. In ten minutes, list as many ideas as you can think of for an oral report on each of the topics you chose. Allow two minutes for each topic.

2. Take five minutes to make a personal victory list. It should be an account of your past successes and stories that you remember well. Add to it regularly. Keep a list of your positive qualities, too. Both these things help you to celebrate your uniqueness.

While you're at it, make a list of topics you know about. This list of topics, like your victory list, will grow as you do. All of these will make for a good speech. If you notice certain things on all your lists, you should give these special consideration. There's probably a whopper of a speech here.

3. Imagine that you have been asked to give a speech or an oral report that has something to do with the general subject of space travel.

First of all, this is a very broad topic. You will want to narrow it down to something more specific that you can talk about. Also remember that it is helpful to begin your research by focusing on a problem—something about space travel that you don't know much about or that would be difficult for scientists to deal with.

Here are some possible topics that are presented as questions that focus on specific problems:

How can astronauts walk in space?
How did scientists develop engines that were
    powerful enough to send rockets into
    space?

How does the space suit protect astronauts and
allow them to go outside the spaceship?

Now see if can think of three more specific topics that
relate to space travel and can be stated as problems: "How
did they do this?" or "What does that mean? or "When did
this happen?"

Finally, pick your own general topic and see if you can
develop at least three specific topics that can be stated as
problems.

4. If you were doing research for an oral report on the
solar system, you might read a paragraph like this in a
textbook or reference book:

> The solar system is made up of the sun
> and a large number of objects that travel in
> orbits around it. Some of these objects are
> no bigger than a grain of sand, but others
> are more than ten times larger than the
> earth. Each of these objects follows an
> elliptical path as it moves around the sun.

What are two of the most important technical terms you
find mentioned here? These are terms that apply specifi-
cally to the solar system; they are not words you are likely
to use in everyday conversation. How would you go about
finding more information on these key terms?

Part Two

Shaping the Speech

Chapter

3

Can I Make a Speech from These Ideas?

There are many ways to construct a speech. In this chapter we will present a simple method, one that has been used by professional and amateur speakers alike. Dr. Snyder has introduced this method in over 600 classrooms from third grade through college. In every case he has helped students overcome their fear of public speaking by teaching them a few basic tricks. This is a simple, yet powerful, formula for giving a speech. If you follow it you will never embarrass yourself, and you may even come to enjoy giving speeches.

You might call this chapter *A Beginners Guide to Constructing a Speech.* We use specific building blocks, just as a contractor does when constructing a house. When these blocks are properly placed together, we achieve the desired result — a solid, well-organized speech.

It is important to remember that in preparing and giving a speech, you are really doing three things:

1. **researching** your topic;
2. **organizing** the information in a speech format; and
3. **delivering** your information to an audience.

You will not be adept at any of the three at first. Remember the helpful words of world-famous speaker Zig Ziglar: Anything worth doing is worth doing poorly until you can learn to do it well. Success is never permanent and failure is never fatal. School is — and should be — a learning laboratory. It is a time for you to take risks and learn how to do new things. Adopt an *I'll try* attitude and let's see what happens.

Now that you have (1) picked your topic and (2) gathered the information for your speech, you are halfway done. But don't worry; now comes the fun part: (3) organizing your information into a usable speech format and (4) giving the speech.

Don't Do It

There are two major pitfalls that many beginning speakers fall into at this point. One is writing the speech out word for word. The other is attempting to memorize the speech.

Written-Out Speech

Once you commit the considerable time and energy to writing your speech out word for word, you are left with only two choices for the presentation of the speech — reading it or delivering a memorized version. Both options lead to poor presentations.

A sure way to bore your audience is to read your speech. It won't take long before most of your listeners' minds start to wander. They will be wishing that you would just give them a copy of your speech and let them read it for themselves. In Chapter 7 we will provide you with six presentation techniques that can make any speech interesting and dynamic. It will be extremely difficult, if not impossible, to use these techniques if you are reading your speech. Another disadvantage of reading your speech is that it gives your audience the impression that you don't really know your material, and therefore you must read it.

A Memorized Speech

If you write your speech out but don't read it, the only other option is memorization. At first this may seem like a good idea. "Hey, if I memorize my speech I'll really know it." It's a temptation you want to avoid for the following reasons:

1. You've wasted your time and energy — Memorizing your speech takes a lot of time and energy. As a speaker, learn to focus your energies outward on the audience, not inwardly on memorization.

2. It is difficult to memorize longer speeches — It's fairly simple to memorize a poem, a few lines in a play or a one- to two-minute speech. Once your speech becomes more then a few minutes in length, however, memorizing it becomes an extremely difficult task. When it comes time to give your speech and you begin to look into the eyes of a live audience, there are too many other things to concentrate on. These get in the way of your ability to recall the memorized text. At some time in your life you will be required to give a much longer presentation. It may be in school, at church, in college, through your job or through organizations you may join. Some of these speeches or

presentations will be thirty minutes, an hour, or even longer. Can you imagine the energy drain of attempting to memorize such a speech?

3. Memorizing your speech increases nervousness — At first thought it would seem that memorizing your speech would make you seem less nervous. "Great, I know my speech word for word. What more could I want?" Actually, just the opposite is true. Instead of allowing your nervous energy to work for you and flow out to the audience, it will stay bottled up inside and build because your main focus will be on recalling each and every word of your speech.

4. Memorization leads to the robot effect — With a memorized speech, you may be looking out at the audience, but you won't really see individuals or interact with them. You will be focusing inward, deep in recall. You will feel like and project yourself like a programmed robot. To many of the people in the audience, you will look programmed.

The difference can be enormous. A live speaker has vitality and is spontaneous. You will project your personality, your insights. YOU are the message. Dr. Snyder's experience as a professional speaker has taught him that only about fifteen percent of the impact you make on an audience is based on your material. (Other professional speakers claim it's as little as seven percent.) Eighty-five percent or more of the impact you make on an audience is based on the way YOU present the material.

We could give two speakers the same material. One might present it in a very interesting, easy-to-understand speech. The other could make the speech totally boring and confusing. I've seen it happen. The success of your speech depends on giving the audience YOU.

The S-MAP: A Speaker's Power Tool

By now you probably agree that reading or memorizing a speech is not in the best interest of the speaker or the audience. But, you ask, what's the alternative? The answer is a simple plan called the Speaker's Master Action Plan, or as we like to call it, the S-MAP. Here's the formula:

$$S + MAP = YOU = SPEAKING\ SUCCESS$$

The S-MAP, like any good map, guides you through new territory. In this case, it helps you to navigate your way through the material you want to present in your speech. It allows you to be spontaneous and give the audience YOU.

Below is a copy of the S-MAP. Notice how it is divided into three simple but necessary parts... the opening, the body, and the close. Under each one there are several building blocks that enable you to select what you need for a well-organized speech.

The Speaker's Master Action Plan (S-MAP)

TOPIC   _____

TITLE   _____

Opening

    Grabber   _____

    WIIFM   _____

(continued on next page)

(continued)

Body

Main Idea **A** _____

    Detail 1 _____

    Detail 2 _____

    Detail 3 _____

Main Idea **B** _____

    Detail 1 _____

    Detail 2 _____

    Detail 3 _____

Main Idea **C** _____

    Detail 1 _____

    Detail 2 _____

    Detail 3 _____

Close

    Summary _____

    Grabber _____

    CTA _____

As you can see from Figure 2, the S-MAP has three major building blocks: the opening, the body, and the close. Each of these is composed of smaller building blocks. Below is the sequence and a brief definition of each one.

The Opening

Grabber is a fact, story, joke, or prop that seizes the audience's attention.

WIIFM stands for What's In It For Me, with "me" being the audience. This lets the listeners know how they will benefit by listening. It is wise to remember that all people want success.

The Body

Main points - these are the major parts of the topic the speaker wants to cover.

Details - these are facts, figures and other bits of information that support and expand the main points.

The Close

Summary - restating the main points to remind the audience what the speaker covered.

A Second Grabber - same as above. A grabber here is optional but it's a nice way to leave the audience with something to think about.

CTA - stands for Call To Action. This is where the speaker challenges or encourages the audience to take some form of action based on the information the speaker has presented.

The **S-MAP** helps you to:

- Organize the presentation.
- Make sure the speech contains the necessary ingredients of a good presentation.
- Save time and energy as you learn your speech.

In the following chapters we will explain the purpose and importance of the key components of the S-MAP, the Opening, the Body, and the Close. In an S-MAP, write only key words which prompt your memory. Do not write in complete sentences; simply use key words and phrases. On the next four pages you will find completed S-Maps that were used for speeches on Pet Peeves and on Ventriliquism.

Remember: The key is to put as few words as possible on the Speaker's MAP and to use them only as a reminder of what you want to say. If, in practicing from your S-MAP, your speech does not come out the same each time — that's good. It will keep getting better. Just as we don't want you to write out your entire speech and read it, don't be tied to your S-MAP. The audience wants YOU. Use your S-MAP only as a guide and to organize your thoughts.

An Example of a Completed S-MAP

TOPIC	PET PEEVES
TITLE	The Pet You Love To Hate
Opening	
Grabber	Fuzzy Puppet
WIIFM	Learn to recognize and even profit from Pet Peeves.
Body	
Main Idea **A**	Advertising jingles that get stuck in your head
Detail 1	Payless - Merry Christmas from Payless
Main Idea **B**	People who sneeze on you
Main Idea **C**	Phone Peeves
Detail 1	ON HOLD
Detail 2	Spell N... A... M... E...
Close	
Summary	
Grabber	People who talk too much - TAPE. (Optional)
CTA	Don't get mad — FIND SOLUTION.

The Pet You Love to Hate

(Christi, a fifth-grade girl, stands before the class with a furry hand puppet on her left hand.)

You may not know it, but you all have a pet peeve. No, it's not a cute, fuzzy little animal (Speaker caresses the puppet) that you buy in the pet store, but something that really bugs you.

It's like when you put your last dime in a coke machine. (Speaker pantomimes.) You're absolutely dying of thirst. You push the button and nothing happens.

A solution to that problem might be to put a sign on the coke machine that says, "If I fail to work, please kick me here." (Speaker holds up sign.)

Many people have profited from the inventions they have made to solve their pet peeves. An example would be the man who got tired of eating stale sandwiches for lunch every single day. He invented the Zip-lock baggy (Speaker shows baggie) and became a millionaire in the process. The Zip-lock baggy has touched many people's lives, (Speaker makes cuddly gesture) and now we don't have to suffer from stale sandwiches any longer.

Here are some examples of my pet peeves. First, advertisements that get stuck in your head like (Speaker holds head in exasperation as she sings jingle) "Merry Christmas from Payless, Merry Christmas from Payless."

Secondly, people who get behind you in line at the grocery store or somewhere else, and they sneeze on you and you can feel a fine mist of sneeze droplets settle on your bare arm and neck. (With right hand speaker makes sprinkling motion over her left arm.)

Then there are my telephone pet peeves. (Speaker makes gesture of holding phone to her ear.) You know, like when you call somewhere and before you can say a word, the person says, "Can you please hold?" I want to say, "Sure, hold what?" And then finally when you do talk to the person and give your name, the person asks, "Can you spell that?" I want to say, "Well - yes, - I - have - been - able - to - spell - my - name - since - kin-der-gar-ten."

Here's a solution I thought of for one of my pet peeves, people who talk too much. (Speaker holds roll of tape.)

So, the next time you're really peeved about something, don't get mad; think of a solution or an invention. Who knows, you might not only help mankind but you may just become the next millionaire.

Another Example of a Finished S-MAP

TOPIC   VENTRILOQUISM
TITLE   How to Become a Ventriloquist
Opening
  Grabber   Lambchop© Puppet 1

WIIFM	Fun — Entertain Friends — Occupation

Body

Main Idea **A**	Getting Started
Detail 1	Take Class - If Available
Detail 2	Library
Detail 3	Magic With Your Voice
Main Idea **B**	Basic Techniques
Detail 1	Breathe Quickly
Detail 2	Vowels — A... E... I... O... U...
Detail 3	Difficult Letters — W... B... F... V... M...
Main Idea **C**	Puppet and Voice
Detail 1	Type — Sock, Stuffed, Wooden
Detail 2	Must have movable mouth
Detail 3	Match voice to puppet
Detail 4	Tip — move mouth for each syllable

Close

Summary	Library — Puppet — Voice — Practice
Grabber	Sadie (Optional)
CTA	Try It.

[see page 6 for the speech based on this S-MAP.]

Let's Talk

The most effective means of communication is conversation, something we all do every day. The S-MAP allows you the freedom to have a conversation with your audience. By using the S-MAP you aren't tied into exact wording or phrases. You simply organize your ideas and share them in a conversation with your audience. YOU give the audience YOU.

Whether you have an audience of five or five hundred people, think of the entire audience as one person. Then, think of that one person as your best friend and you are merely having a conversation with that one friend. This technique helps to take away the fear of speaking in front of large audiences.

As you practice your speech using the S-MAP, you won't say it exactly the same every time. That's good. Each time you practice it will get better since you'll be free to make adjustments. The read or memorized speech always stays the same.

Many times in Dr. Snyder's communication courses, even after all this advice, a student will get up and read his or her first speech. Such was the case of Frank, a tenth-grader.

Frank loved volcanoes; he lived for volcanoes. He's even visited a few, including Mount St. Helens. After high school he wanted to study geology. Guess what Frank's first speech was about?

Volcanoes you say? Lucky guess! Sounds like a great choice. Frank knew his subject; as a matter of fact, he had a passion for it. Sounds like a formula for a super speech, right? It should've been — but it wasn't.

Frank wrote his speech and then read it word for word. Just seconds into the speech, classmates were beginning to squirm. Some gazed at the posters hanging on the walls, a few doodled, most were staring blankly at their desks. Practically no one was watching Frank, but he didn't notice. His eyes were glued to his paper and his voice droned on in monotone. A good topic and good material turned into a bad speech.

Frank was glad when it was time to sit down so he could finally put himself and his audience out of their misery. Still, you could see the disappointment in his eyes. He no sooner took his seat than Dr. Snyder asked him to return to the lectern.

"Frank, I know that you know a lot about volcanoes. If I were to come over to your house after school, how long could you talk with me about volcanoes?" Dr. Snyder asked.

"Mmmm… Probably about an hour, hour and a half," Frank replied.

"I'm sure," said Dr. Snyder. "I want you to have some of that same talk right now with your classmates. Let's take just a moment and organize it. What are three key ideas you know about volcanoes?"

"Well, I know what causes them to erupt, and… I know about some of the more famous volcanoes… and let's see… "

"You said you had visited Mt. St. Helens. Could you tell us what that was like?" Dr. Snyder asked.

"Sure," Frank responded.

"Well there you have your three main points: A, B, and C."

- What causes volcanoes to erupt
- Famous volcanoes
- My visit to Mt. St. Helens

"Now using these main points, please give us a little talk about volcanoes."

Frank proceeded to "have a conversation" with his audience about volcanoes. This time he had everyone's undivided attention. He explained in his own words what caused volcanic eruptions and even drew a diagram on the chalkboard. He next talked about some of the more famous volcanoes, and told what made them famous. Frank even retrieved a book from his desk, one he had used as a reference, and showed a few pictures.

By now his classmates were hooked. Frank finished by sharing the experiences he had visiting Mt. St. Helens. He even challenged the audience to learn more about this wonder of nature and gave them the titles of some good books on the subject. Frank also reminded them that Ring of Fire, a documentary about volcanoes, was playing at the local I-MAX theater.

By now Frank had by far surpassed his allotted time, but nobody seemed to mind. In fact, many students had questions. Dr. Snyder reminded the class it was necessary to move on to the next speaker. Frank returned to his seat, but this time he walked a little taller. The disappointment on his face was replaced by a look of satisfaction.

"Frank, all you have to do is add a grabber and a WIIFM and you have one dynamite speech."

His classmates nodded in agreement. They were all beginning to see how "having a conversation" with the audience really worked.

This story about Frank is true, but not unique. Dr. Snyder encounters this situation on a daily basis. Each time the speaker is asked to return to the front of the class. The speaker and Dr. Snyder, sometimes with the help of the class, come up with three main points. The speaker then "talks" to the audience about the topic. The speaker and the audience are always amazed at the sudden drastic improvement.

Why Use the Speaker's MAP?

In the back of this book we provide a black-line master of our Speaker's MAP for you to copy and use in preparing a speech. Use it instead of note cards. Why, you ask? Learn to love your S-MAP. It has many advantages over any other type of speech construction.

The S-MAP is the Checklist.

The S-MAP serves as a checklist to make sure you've included all the necessary building blocks of a successful speech.

The S-MAP is better than a written out speech.

If you write out your speech word for word, as already mentioned, you will do one of two things. You will either read it (boring) or you will memorize it (big waste of time and energy). Conversation is the most relaxing and effective form of communication. We want you to have a conversation with your audience. The Speaker's MAP only serves as your notes to be sure you cover everything you want to say in your conversation.

The S-MAP is better than note cards.

Dr. Snyder knows many professional speakers who use note cards to prepare and deliver a speech. Note cards have no advantages and several distinct disadvantages compared with an S-MAP. First of all, if you speak very often, sooner or later you are going to drop your note cards on the floor. Funny thing: They never fall in order. Hopefully you have numbered them and thus minimize the shuffling and reshuffling necessary to get back on track. If your S-MAP falls on the floor, simply pick it up and set it back on the lectern. Secondly, turning note cards ties up your hands. This makes it difficult for the speaker to use gestures (pages 134-135).

Finally, using note cards builds anxiety in the speaker. Dr. Snyder speaks from experience. Sometimes you get up to speak and you're all pumped up and you get off to a super start. You're breezing along (even starting to enjoy it) when suddenly a frightening thought enters your mind.

You realize that you've probably already shot past several note cards. You fear that when the time comes and you finally have to glance down, the card that you need will be buried somewhere in the stack. - SOCIAL CATASTERSTROKE.

The S-MAP helps organize impromptu speeches.

We will cover impromptu, or spur-of-the-moment, speaking in Chapter 12. The neat thing about an S-MAP is that you can create one on the spur of the moment, on paper or in your head. One challenge that good speakers often face is when they are asked to speak unexpectedly. It may be at a meeting where the planned speaker fails to show, or there is a change in the program, or some other set of unexpected circumstances. Whatever the reason, most people think that an accomplished speaker can just get up and give a speech. Professionals don't like these situations because, like professionals in all occupations, they believe in being over-prepared. With The S-MAP, however, they can pull it off. So can you.

Chapter

4

Body Building

As you recall from the examples in the last chapter, the S-MAP has three key elements: the opening, the body and the close. Each of these is composed of critical components which we demonstrated in Chapter 3. Below is a reminder of the sequence of the building blocks as they should appear in a speech or presentation.

Opening
Grabber
WIIFM - (What's In It For Me)
Body
Main point A
Details
Main point B
Details
Main point C
Details

Close

Summary

Grabber

CTA (Call To Action)

Each of these building blocks will be covered in detail with examples given in the following chapters.

Constructing a speech has many similarities to constructing a house, a model, or a bridge. Each building block has a specific purpose and place. Obviously with most structures there is a sequence to the order of construction. For example, you can't put the roof on a house before you have built the foundation or the walls. In your finished speech, there is a definite order for how the building blocks should fit together for the best effect. This is clearly presented in the S-MAP.

In constructing your speech, however, you can start anywhere. You may have a great story or a prop that would make a good starting point. You might feel very strongly about an issue and build your speech around a CTA. Your main points may develop first and, later, you can add a Grabber, WIIFM, and the CTA.

In this chapter we are going to start constructing our speech with the second main building block, the body. This is a good place for the beginning speaker to start since it helps to organize the information. We will cover the building blocks of the opening in Chapter 5 and those of the close in Chapter 6. The main thing in successful speech construction is to GET STARTED. Don't suffer the paralysis of over analysis. It doesn't matter WHERE you start ... but START.

The body of the speech contains most of the actual information you want to present to the audience about your topic. Almost all of the information you have gathered in your research will be in this section. The best way to organize the body is through main points. This helps to organize your speech for the audience so that it is easy for them to follow along. This also helps to organize the speech for the speaker so it is easy to remember. You will notice in the S-MAP there is room for three main points. This seems to be the best number for speaker and listener alike. That is not to say that your speech can not have just two main points or four main points. What you want to avoid is having too many main points. This confuses and over-whelms the listener.

One of the biggest mistakes that most speakers make is trying to give the audience too much information at one time. For example, if I started my speech on study skills by saying, "There are twenty-six things you can do to get an A in math," I would immediately see my audience start to tune out. They would be thinking "I can't even remember twenty-six things, let alone do them." However, if I say, "Today I am going to share with you the top three things you can do to get an A in math this year" — what a difference! I have now captured their interest because they feel there is a much greater chance that they will be able to follow through on three tips.

Developing Main Points

There are two approaches you can take in preparing the body of your speech. In one approach you organize your main points first and then conduct the necessary research to provide accurate supporting details. This is called the organize-research approach. In the second approach, you research your topic first. Then you organize your speech and choose your main points based on the information you have gathered. This is called the research-organize approach. Let's examine each.

Organize-Research

In the Organize-Research approach you are developing a speech on a topic you already feel comfortable with. Since you already possess a great deal of information, you need to research only to develop a key idea more fully or to make sure of your accuracy. The key step in this method is to select the three main points (A, B, and C) to present.

Research-Organize

This method is recommended if you must speak on a subject you are not very familiar with. This is usually an assignment where considerable research will be necessary. With the research-organize approach, you gather as much information as you can about your topic. When researching, follow the steps in Chapter 2. Group details of information that are related to one another. Finally, select the three groups that contain the most information that would make for an informative and interesting speech. These become your main points. You may have to leave out some interesting details that don't fit into these three main categories. Don't worry. It is important not to overwhelm the audience with too much information. Your goal is to deliver a well-organized speech that the audience can understand. Let's look at how we might use either of these approaches.

Using the Organize-Research Method

If you know your topic well and have considerable prior knowledge, the organize-research method is the one to use. With a little practice, you will be surprised how easy it is to break topics into three main points. Below are some examples.

Topic: **Collecting Baseball Cards**

A   How to get started.
B   Protecting your cards.
C   Pricing your cards.

Topic: **The Greenhouse Effect**

A   What is it?

B   Why is it a problem?

C   What can we do to solve this problem?

Topic: **Medieval Castles**

A   When and why were they built?

B   Where were they built?

C   What the typical castle was like.

There is no one way to break a topic into its main points. If we were to give ten students the same topic and have them develop three main points, it is very possible we could have ten very different S-MAPs.

Topic: **Cats**

Student One

A   Brief History

B   House Cats

C   Wild Cats

Student Two

A   Choosing a Cat

B   Caring For a Cat

C   Fun Things You Can Do with Your Cat

Student Three

A   Morris

B   Garfield

C   Heathcliff

When Dr. Snyder first started speaking, he tried to make an acronym with his main points. This really helped him remember them and in their proper order. For example, one speech he gave was about the ABC's of success.

A - Attitude (Positive thinking)
B - Backbone (Hard work)
C - Commitment (Keep improving)

You can see that he stretched things a little to fit the ABC patterns, but it worked. In another early speech, Dr. Snyder used the acronym SHIP. In this presentation, he used four main parts but kept them simple and brief. This speech dealt with the ingredients that it takes to live a successful life. The body of the speech looked like this on his S-MAP:

TOPIC   Ingredients for a Successful Life

Main Idea	Acronym. Word It Stands For	
A	S	Self Esteem
B	H	Hard Work
C	I	Itinerary
D	P	Persistence

Maybe he stretched it with the word *itinerary*, which means to have an agenda or a plan. Of course he was careful to explain the meaning of this word to the audience. In the end, they had a SHIP. He explained to the audience how each member was the captain of his or her own ship. If they followed the principles that he had presented, they would be sailing toward the port named Success.

Let's look at a few more examples of how the organize-research method was used. The example of the speech on ventriloquism (pages 6–9) was constructed using the organize-research method. Once Jessica chose the topic, she quickly decided on the three main points:

A. Getting Started
B. Techniques
C. Puppet-voice

She then filled in the details with the information she knew under each of the main points. Her S-MAP can be seen on pages 60–61.

Let's look at a second example. Here is Christi's speech on Pet Peeves from Chapter 3 (pages 59–60). Once she chose pet peeves as her topic, she asked herself what were three pet peeves she could use as main points. She chose:

A. Jingles that stick in your head
B. People who sneeze on you
C. Telephone pet peeves

Now let's see how Christi developed her S-Map:

Christi's S-MAP

TOPIC	PET PEEVES
TITLE	The Pet You Love To Hate
Opening	
Grabber	Fuzzy Puppet
WIIFM	Learn to recognize and even profit from Pet Peeves.
Body	
Main Idea **A**	Advertising jingles that get stuck in your head
Detail 1	Payless - Merry Christmas from Payless
Main Idea **B**	People who sneeze on you
Main Idea **C**	Phone Peeves
Detail 1	ON HOLD
Detail 2	Spell N... A... M... E...

Close
    Summary
    Grabber   People who talk too much - TAPE.
                    (Optional)
    CTA   Don't get mad — FIND SOLUTION.

Using the Research-Organize Method

The organize-research method is a great help when the speaker doesn't have a lot of prior knowledge about the topic and needs to do considerable research. This is often the case with an assigned a topic. Then the research must be done first. Here are a few examples.

Assigned topic: CASTLES

Most were built A.D. 500-1400 -
    Middle Ages
over 10,000 built in Germany alone
built throughout Europe, Russia, Syria,
    Turkey, Jordan
 800 - Germany- wooden towers
 1066 - Eng. Wm. the Conqueror-
mote(mound) and bailey (oval courtyard)
siege strategies:
battering ram
catapult
mine/tunnel

Parts
outer wall(curtain) 300 ft. ea. side, 20 ft.
    high, 8ft. thick
synonym:outerward
inner wall(curtain)200 ft. ea. side 35 ft.
    high, 12 ft. thick
 synonym: innerward

Great Hall 35 x100 ft.-meals, entertainment, gathering place
towers
dungeon- inner tower of inner curtain
towers-10 ft. higher than curtains
trench- water or dry
drawbridge
orig. for defense
later used for country homes
early Eng. def. against Vikings
900 in Belguim alone
1100's and 1200's- brick and stone replaces
  wood
Royal castles-king, strategic locations
  throughout kingdom
baronial castles-baron, lord used to defend
  fief-feudal system
dogs/cats allowed to roam to keep rodent
  pop. down
by 1500 demise-centralized govt. in many
  countries therefore less fighting among
  kings and lords
gunpowder and cannons
picture of stone castle
picture of mote and bailey castle
diagram of castle floor plan
pictures of battering ram and catapult

These facts were gathered in a two-hour trip to the
library. Now that we have collected them, how can we use
them? Remember we do not want to overwhelm the audience. We need to make sense of what we have and select
three main points to develop. Therefore, some of these facts
will have to be ignored.

Now let's see how these facts might be grouped under headings in an attempt to create main points.

HISTORY
most built A. D. 500-1400 -Middle Ages
over 10,000 in Germany alone
found in Europe, Russia, Syria, Turkey, and Jordan
900 in Belgium
originally for defense
later used for country homes
Royal- king, strategic location
baronial- baron, lord- defend fief- feudal system
early Eng. kings defended against Vikings

TYPES
wooden towers- Germany-800's
1066 Wm. the Conq.- trench(mound) and bailey(oval courtyard)
1200's- stone or brick
picture of trench and bailey castle
pictures of stone castle

SIEGE
battering ram
mine
siege towers
catapult
cut off supplies - starvation
picture of battering ram
picture of catapult

PHYSICAL FEATURES - typical castle
outer curtain (300 ft. ea. side, 20 ft. h, 8 ft. thick)
outer ward

inner curtain (200 ft. ea. side, 35 ft. h, 12 ft. thick)
inner ward
great hall (35 ft. wide X 100 ft. long)
dungeon
drawbridge
towers on outer curtain =10 ft. higher
towers on inner curtain = 35 ft. higher
moat wet or dry
floor plan of typical castle

We now have all our information grouped under main headings. Often bits of information seem to stand alone; that is, they don't seem to fit in with any of the other facts. These facts can be grouped under a *miscellaneous* heading. In this example all of our facts grouped nicely under four main headings. It is possible to have considerably more. From our main headings we will develop the **main points** of our speech. To do this, ask three questions:

- Which main headings contain the most information?
- Which main headings contain the most interesting information?
- Which main headings seem to fit together best?

This is a very important step in the construction of your speech. Not only will you be deciding which information you will **use,** but just as important, you will be deciding which information you will **lose** (speaker's lingo for discard). **Don't be afraid to get rid of information !!!** You can't tell your audience everything about your subject in one speech. It may be necessary to discard entire headings to limit yourself to just three or four. Once you have selected the main headings you will use for your **main**

points, you may need to discard some of this information also.

An Example of an S-MAP on Castles

TOPIC	Castles
TITLE	Home Sweet Home in the Middle Ages
Opening	
Grabber	Old saying-close eyes-Merlin costume
WIIFM	Learn more about castles
Body	
Main Idea **A**	History
Detail 1	Most built A.D. 500-1400 - Middle Ages
Detail 2	Many built - 10,000 Germany alone
Detail 3	Defense, English vs Vikings
Detail 4	Baronial, Royal - feudalism
Main Idea **B**	Types
Detail 1	Wooden - typical in Germany - 800's
Detail 2	Mote and bailey - 1066, Wm. the Conqueror (picture)
Detail 3	Stone castle - 1200's (pictures)
Main Idea **C**	Features (show floor plan)
Detail 1	Drawbridge - moat
Detail 2	Outer curtain - 300 ft. x 20 ft. x 8 ft., tower 10 ft. higher
Detail 3	Inner curtain - 200 ft. x 35 ft. x 12 ft. tower 50 ft. higher
Detail 4	Great hall - 100 ft. x 35 ft.
Detail 5	Dungeon - bottom of inner tower
Main Idea **D**	Strategy against
Detail 1	Direct attack
Detail 2	Siege

Close
    Summary   Repeat main ideas A - B - C - D
    Grabber   (Student did not use)
    CTA   Visit Royal Library... visit castles

Notice how the speaker used four **main points, A, B, C** and **D.** "Let's see how Tom developed his speech."

Home Sweet Home in the Middle Ages

There's an old saying that a man's home is his castle. Well, there was a time period in history, The Middle Ages, when many people actually did live in castles. Close your eyes for a moment. We are about to enter a time machine. Destination: The Middle Ages.

Ah, we've arrived. We find ourselves not only in the middle of the Middle Ages, but smack dab in the middle of the great hall of a huge castle. Merlin the Mentor is gathering his students around him. They are seated on wooden benches around a long wooden table. The wise old scholar is about to begin a lecture on — of all subjects — castles. Open your eyes. If we hurry we can join them. (When the students open their eyes, they find Tom has put on a Middle Ages costume and a white beard while their eyes were closed. He now takes on the persona of Merlin the Mentor). **(Grabber)**

Today students, I am going to share with you some knowledge of one of the greatest inventions of all time, the castle. **(WIIFM for**

Tom's audience as well as Merlin's students.) First I'm going to tell you a little
about the history of the castle **(A)**. Then we
will learn about different types of castles
(B); the layout of the typical castle **(C)** and
finally we will discuss some of the strategies
enemies have used against castles **(D)**.

First let's look at the history of these
architectural giants. Most castles were built
between A.D 500 and 1400, a period known
as the Middle Ages. During this period
castles were built throughout all of Europe,
Russia, and the Middle East. Castles were a
lot more common than most people realize.
It is estimated that over 10,000 castles were
built in Germany alone.

Originally castles were built for defense.
The early English kings constructed them as
a defense against Viking invasions. Baronial
castles were built by barons, lords, and
other rulers of prominence to defend their
fief, or ruling domain as it was known. This
was the basis of the feudal system that was
the predominant system of government
throughout Europe during the Middle Ages.
Whereas baronial castles were built on the
specific land of the ruler, royal castles were
those built by kings at strategic locations
throughout the kingdom.

One of the fascinating things about
castles is their uniqueness. No two castles
are exactly alike. Most castles do fit into one
of three main types, depending mostly on

the period during which they were built. The earliest type of castle was basically a wooden fence with wooden towers. These were typical of the castles built in Germany in the 800's.

After 1066 William the Conqueror introduced the mote and bailey castle. The main part of this castle was built on top of a small hill or mound (mote). From this central structure a stockade-like fence branched out encircling a large courtyard known as the bailey. The mote and bailey castle became the prominent type of castle throughout Europe, and over the next 200 years literally thousands were built. (Tom showed a picture of a mote and bailey castle.)

By the 1200's mote and bailey castles started being replaced by the elaborate stone structures we know as castles today. (Here Tom shows several pictures of stone castles.) Although each stone castle was unique in architecture, design, and size, they all had many common features. I will take you on a brief tour of the typical stone castle.(Here Tom displays a poster showing a castle floor plan.) We enter the castle through a lowered drawbridge. This bridge can be raised in a matter of moments by a series of pulleys should the need arise. When lowered, the bridge spans a moat, which is a deep dug-out trench that sur-rounds the castle. The moat may or may not be filled with water. The purpose of the moat is to make an attack on the castle very difficult.

As we cross the drawbridge, we enter the main gate in the outer wall, which is known as the outer curtain. The outer curtain is 300 ft. long on each side, about the length of a football field. The outer curtain wall is 20 ft. high and 8 ft. thick. At intervals along the length of the outer wall are towers that rise an additional 10 ft. These serve as watch towers during battle. Inside the outer wall is an inner wall or inner curtain. The inner curtain serves as a second line of defense and protects all of the structures that are vital to the castles survival. It's almost like having a castle within a castle. The inner curtain is 200 ft. in length on each side, 35 ft. high and 12 ft. thick. The towers along the inner curtain rose an additional 50 ft. This enabled defenders manning these towers to shoot over the outer curtain.

Two other structures typical of most castles are the Great Hall and the dungeon. The Great Hall was the center of activity inside the castle. It is 35 ft. wide and 100 ft. long. It serves as the general gathering and dining area for the entire population of the castle. The dungeon is usually built in the bottom of one of the towers of the inner curtain. This is where criminals, prisoners of war, and those disloyal to the king will be jailed.

Castles are extremely effective in defending the land and protecting its subjects. There are only two possible strategies that can be used to conquer castles. One is a direct attack on the castle. This is rarely successful and requires a huge army. Some special weapons have been developed to help such an attack. This is a picture of a battering ram (Tom shows). It is used to smash the gates. Here is a picture of a catapult (Tom displays). It was developed to launch stones, fireballs, and other objects over the castle walls.

The second strategy employed against castles has a greater chance of success but requires a lot more time and patience. This is the siege. Here the invading force simply sets up camp outside the castle walls and waits for the inhabitants inside to run out of supplies, especially food and water. Both strategies fail more often than they succeed.

So, my students, in today's lesson we have taken a brief introductory look at these wonderful structures we call castles. We have discussed the history of castles, types of castles, some of the physical features, and strategies used against castles.

(Summary). I hope you will visit the Royal Library and read a little more on this subject. You may also plan to visit other castles if your travels permit.

(CTA) You are dismissed for the noon meal, but let's assemble promptly at one o'clock for Sorcery 101.

Remember Sharon, who was mentioned in Chapter 2? She was assigned a speech in science class. The only restriction was that it had to have something to do with genetics, and she chose twins as a topic. Let's see how Sharon used her research (pp. 39-44) to construct a speech. She decided to develop her ABC from the following main headings:

> **A** = How Twins Form
> **B** = Interesting Facts about Twins
> **C** = Interview

She then decided to construct a **grabber** from the information under the Famous Twins heading. That left the headings *Types of Twins, Siamese Twins,* and *Miscellaneous* not being used. She felt she could combine some of the material in the *Types of Twins* under the *How Twins Form* heading. Sharon felt the information under the *Siamese Twins* heading was extremely interesting, so she decided to use it as part of the *Interesting Facts About Twins* heading.

Let's see how the S-MAP developed.

TOPIC	Twins
TITLE	Double the Trouble or Twice as Nice
Opening	
Grabber	Romulus & Remus, Gemini, MN baseball team, and Pauline Esther & Esther Pauline Friedman
WIIFM	Journey through Wonder World of Twins

Body

Main Idea **A**	How twins form
Detail 1	<u>Identical</u> - one egg (embryo) splits in two - look alike, odds = 1/300
Detail 2	<u>fraternal</u> - two eggs develop at same time - may or may not be same sex, don't look exactly alike
Detail 3	born few weeks early, <6 lbs. vs >7 lbs.
Main Idea **B**	Interesting facts
Detail 1	Mother of twins more likely to have twins again -Mrs. M.L. Pearson of Florida - 7 sets
Detail 2	One twin born first. <u>Guess</u> longest time between births - <u>147 days</u>
Detail 3	Egg (embryo) splitting early - identical twins later - mirror image twins latest - Siamese twins
Detail 4	Siamese twins - Chang & Eng - born Thailand (Siam) 1811, moved to US. - joined circus, married sisters = 22 children, died 1874 -3 hrs. apart
Main Idea **C**	Interview
Detail 1	Dan & Dave Rice - 10 yrs.
Detail 2	Switched classes - 4th & 5th grades
Detail 3	Appendix story

Detail 4	Enjoy - camaraderie and attention, Don't like - being grouped together and identity mix ups

Close

Summary	Repeat A - B - C - D
Grabber	Famous Friedman twins, Dear Ann & Dear Abby-Kate & Duplicate
CTA	*Twins* by Jay Ingram - take my advice

And here's the speech:

Double Trouble or Twice as Nice?

Do you know what Romulus and Remus, Gemini, the Minnesota baseball team, and Pauline Esther and Esther Pauline Friedman have in common? If you said they are all famous twins, you are absolutely right. Romulus and Remus, of course, are the twin brothers credited with founding Rome. Gemini is the twin constellation and also the sign of the twin on the astrological chart. And of course, unless you've been living in a cave, everyone knows the famous Friedman twins. **(Grabber). You don't?** Well don't worry, you soon will. You will also learn a lot of other interesting things about twins. So fasten your seat belts because we are about to take a fascinating journey through the wonderful world of twins. **(WIIFM).** On this journey you will learn how twins form **(A),** some interesting facts about twins **(B),** and I will share the results of an interview with the twins who live next door (**C**). And... I'll share the identity of the famous Friedman twins.

First let's look at how twins form in the womb. There are two types of twins, identical twins and fraternal twins. They form quite differently. Identical twins are exactly that: identical. The reason they are identical is because they come from the same fertilized egg. For some reason that still has scientists puzzled, very early in its development the fertilized egg, or embryo, splits in two. Each of these parts develops into a baby. With two growing babies, naturally it gets a little crowded in the mother's womb. This is why twins are usually born a few weeks earlier than most babies and usually weigh a little less. Most twins at birth weigh a little less than 6 pounds. Non-twin babies, on average, weigh a little more than 7 pounds. The probability of being born an identical twin is about 1/300. Even at these odds there are approximately 30 million sets of twins world wide.

The second type of twins are called fraternal twins. Here two babies form in the womb at the same time, but from two different eggs. Having the same father and mother, these twins of course, share many of the same genes but they are not identical. They may or may not look alike, they are about as similar as normal siblings not born at the same time. They may be brothers, sisters, or brother and sister.

There have been many studies about twins and many interesting facts have been recorded. For example, mothers who have twins are more likely to have twins again. Mrs. M. L. Pearson of Florida has had seven sets of twins. When twins are born, by necessity, one twin is always born first. The second twin usually follows a few moments later. Would anyone like to guess the longest length of time between arrivals?

(The speaker asked for guesses here.)

Believe it or not, the answer is 147 days.

Another unusual thing about twins is that, depending at what stage the embryo splits, the results can be dramatically differ-ent. If the embryo splits early, identical twins will result. If the embryo splits a little later in its development, mirror image twins result. One twin looks like the mirror image of the other. For example, if one twin has a dimple on the right cheek, the other will have a dimple on the same spot only on the left cheek. If the split is very late, a phenom-enon called Siamese twins result. In this case the embryo does not completely split and the babies are born joined together. Sometimes only tissue and cartilage hold them together and the babies can be surgi-cally separated. If vital organs are shared, if separated, one twin will usually die.

The term Siamese twins comes from two twins, Chang and Eng. They were born in 1811 in Thailand, which was then known as Siam. They moved to the United States and made their living working for the circus as a main attraction. Chang and Eng married sisters and between them had 22 children. Although they were joined throughout their entire lives, the twins maintained separate homes several miles apart. They would spend three days at one house and then three days at the other. Chang and Eng died in 1874 within three hours of each other.

Probably everyone in our class has seen at least one set of twins in their lifetime. A few of you may even know some twins personally. I'm one of those fortunate ones. Dan and Dave Rice, ten-year-old twins, are my next-door neighbors. I thought it would be neat to interview them as part of my research. They had a lot of interesting experiences to share. On two occasions, once in fourth grade and once in fifth, they switched classrooms. None of the teachers and only a handful of their friends caught on. When they were seven, Dave had acute appendicitis, and was rushed to the emergency room. Two hours later while Dave's appendix was being removed, Dan, sitting at home felt some pain in the same spot.

Dan and Dave enjoy being twins, although it has its drawbacks. They enjoy the companionship and all the attention they get. Sometimes they resent the lack of identity, always being grouped together, and having people getting mixed up. As Dan put it "It makes you stop and think when your own Mom isn't sure who you are".

Today we have covered how twins form, some interesting facts about twins, and we've looked at what it's actually like to be a twin. The subject of twins is not only fascinating, but scientists feel learning more about twins can be valuable. It just might unlock many of the mysteries about genetics and heredity. If you would like to learn more about twins, there are some excellent sources in our school library. One book I found particularly helpful is *Twins* by Jay Ingram. If you read this book you will learn the identity of the famous Friedman twins, but don't worry, I won't make you wait. As youngsters, they were so much alike and so inseparable that their friends called them Kate and Duplicate. Today they are known worldwide as Ann Landers and Abigail van Buren, Dear Ann and Dear Abby. Each day millions of readers take their advice. I hope you'll take my advice and learn more twins. **(CTA)**

Details: The Support Points

Once you have determined what your main points will be (**A, B,** and **C**) you will want to support or build on them by adding **details.** Go back and see how each of the four speeches highlighted in this chapter (pet peeves, ventriloquism, castles, and twins) used details to support and expand its **main points.** Most main points should be supported by two to four details. Supporting details may be statistics, quotes, stories, examples, or any other type of information that backs-up your main idea.

Types of Details

When most people think of details they usually think of facts and figures. Perhaps the encyclopedia is the first source that comes to mind. Encyclopedias and reference books can be excellent sources of details. Don't, however, limit yourself to factual details. Not all details come from reference books. Details gathered from personal experiences are excellent ones and make your speech come alive. Including such details is crucial to telling the whole story. Speakers and writers rely on personal details which are supplied from other sources: their senses (sensory details), memories (memory details), or imaginations (reflective details).

Sensory Details. Use your senses of touch, taste, hearing, vision, and smell. These details are gathered through firsthand experience. By closely observing what is going on around you, you will be able to gather plenty of sensory details about any person, place, or thing you write about. Sensory details become especially important when painting word pictures for the audience. An example: *Terry's father, Mr. Brown, not only looks like a drill sergeant dressed in various shades of army green, he barks like one.*

Memory Details. This type of detail comes from your memory of past experiences. It might be a detail remembered from yesterday or ten years back. A personal journal can play an important role in gathering memory details.

You can get help by checking facts with a family member or an old friend who shared the experience with you. As a matter of fact, it is a good idea to check your own recollection. You will discover that someone else may remember the event a little differently and can fill in the blanks in your memory.

Reflective Details. This type of detail comes to mind when you thnk about a particular event and imagine what might have been or might yet be — what you imagine, wish for, or hope. This type of detail is useful in telling a story and also in enriching a description. An example: *I wonder just how many pull-ups Mr. Brown could do if he were in my shoes.*

Details from Other Sources. When you are asked to write on a topic, gather personal details from what you already know. Then, depending on what you recall, you may have to add details — facts, figures, reasons and examples — which come from other sources. Again, don't limit yourself to reference books and materials alone. Here are some additional ideas of possible resources for obtaining details.

1. Ask another person — a parent, neighbor, friend, teacher — anyone who has the information you need.

2. Ask an expert, or someone who has a lot of experience with your topic. For example if you are thinking about your fear of the dentist, ask a dental assistant for the nuts and bolts of how a tooth is filled, or for the names of the dentist's instruments.

3. You can call (or write for information if you have the time). Learn to use the phone book; it can save you time and effort. A great source is the Reference Librarian at your local library. Part of his or her job is to answer questions by phone.

4. You can gather details in the library. There are magazines, books, videotapes, picture files, and computer research services. Ask the Reference Librarian for help.

We will close this chapter by taking a look at the **S-MAP** of another speech.

Notice how the details were developed and then how they are molded into a speech.

TOPIC	Being a Baseball Fan
TITLE	Baseball and You
Opening	
Grabber	Tired of striking out ?
WIIFM	Easy, fun, exciting - America's favorite pastime
Body	
Main Idea **A**	Choose a team
Detail 1	Pick from hometown, sister - Marlins - likes hats
Detail 2	Watch on TV - Cubs (WGN), Mets (WOR), Braves (WTBS)
Detail 3	ESPN
Detail 4	Sportscenter
Main Idea **B**	Collecting your team's souvenirs
Detail 1	Cards- Two star players
Detail 2	Notebook-1985-1993

Detail 3	Show both caps
Detail 4	T-shirts and shorts
Detail 5	Tomahawk
Main Idea **C**	Baseball terms
Detail 1	Texas League single
Detail 2	sacrifice fly
Detail 3	twin bill / doubleheader
Close	
CTA	Catch the fever

Here's how the speech sounded.

Baseball and You

(David, a sixth-grade boy, stands before the class dressed in an Atlanta Braves T-shirt. To his right is a table filled with various baseball souvenirs.)

Are you tired of striking out with your friends because you don't know all the latest baseball scoops? Well now it's easy to learn a lot about baseball. It's fun and exciting. Besides, it's America's favorite pastime.

First, I recommend you choose a TEAM. (He points to his Atlanta Braves T-shirt.) You'll notice I picked out the Atlanta Braves, not only because I was born there but also because I know a lot about them. You may want to pick out a team from the state where you were born, your hometown, or you can pick out any team at all. My sister likes the Marlins because she likes the color of their hats. Don't worry if they're not a good team like the White Sox, Braves, or Blue Jays. Pick out any team you really like.

Next watch your team on TV. For example, the Braves are on WTBS, the Cubs are on WGN, and the Mets are on WOR. These can be found on most local cable networks. Or you may find a lot of different teams on ESPN or on SPORTSCENTER every night. Don't let anyone influence you on which team to follow. Just pick one and stick with it.

Each team usually has one or two star players you can focus on. My favorite players on the Braves are Dave Justice, Fred McGriff, and Steve Avery. (David shows the audience plastic-covered baseball cards of these players.) I have a whole bunch of their cards which some day may be worth a lot. You'll notice I have a whole notebook that's devoted to the Braves. In it you'll notice I have items and cards acquired between 1985-1993.

You can also collect caps. (David holds up white cap.) This is an Atlanta Braves back-to-back cap which honors their second consecutive National League West Championship won in 1992. (David then holds up a red and blue cap) This is the official Atlanta Braves uniform cap, which they wear when they go onto the field. You can get different T-shirts and shorts to match. (David points to his matching outfit). You can even get the famous Brave tomahawk. (David displays rubber tomahawk and chops through the air.)

Once you've picked out your favorite team and collected the items, you need to learn baseball terms. This is almost like learning a foreign language. For example, you might hear Harry Carey mention that Ryne Sandberg just hit a Texas League single. This means a little pop up just over the infielder's outstretched glove fell in for a hit. Or Vin Scully celebrates Mike Piazza driving in the lead run with a sacrifice fly. This means the batter hit a fly ball to an outfielder, but the runner on third was able to tag-up and score after the catch. A twin bill or doubleheader means that a team is playing two games that day.

Whether you're playing baseball, watching baseball, or collecting baseball souvenirs, there is something for everyone. Catch the fever!

A Final Thought

Let me emphasize two points that are important as you gather information and prepare the body of your speech.

Don't limit yourself to reference books when doing your research. Talk to people! Gather first-hand information, ask for interviews, explore sensory details, memory details, reflective details from many sources.

Put as few words as possible on your S-MAP — just enough to keep you going. Just as important as putting information into your speech is putting YOU into the presentation. Along with the information you will give, that will vitalize your speech.

Remember . . .

Use your **Speaker's MAP** *as a blueprint to organize your presentation.*

Your S-MAP also serves as a checklist to make sure you include all the necessary materials to build a good speech

❖ Now Try This:

Applying What You Have Learned

1. Imagine that you are to give a speech on each of the topics below. On a piece of paper, see how quickly you can develop an A B C (main points) for each subject.

Art	Holidays	Games	School
Food	Music	Discipline	Animals
TV	Books	Hobbies	Travel
People	Places	Current Events	

2. The purpose of this next exercise is to help the speaker organize the body of his or her presentation by using questions.

THE LOTTERY
If you won ten million dollars in the
    lottery…
A. What gift would you give yourself?
B. What gift would you give to a special person
    in your life?
C. What charity would you contribute to?

PROBLEMS AND SOLUTIONS
A. What is the number-one problem facing our
    country?
B. What are some possible solutions?
C. What is the best solution?

GREAT MOMENTS
A. What do you feel is the greatest moment in
    U. S. history?

B. What do you feel is the saddest moment in U. S. history?

C. What is your favorite moment in U. S. history?

YOUR SCHOOL

A. Share something that you really like about your school.

B. Share something that you don't like about your school.

C. How would you improve it?

Chapter

5

Great Beginnings

In this chapter we will explore a simple but effective method to develop the **opening** of your speech. In speechmaking, it is essential to get off to a good start. You must get the attention of your audience right from the beginning. In today's hi-tech, fast-paced world, you will find that audiences make snap decisions. Studies show that speakers must seize or "grab" the attention of the audience within the first 60 seconds. I have observed that speakers who successfully gain the audience's attention early usually hold their attention throughout the speech — even if the presentation gets worse.

On the other hand, if the speaker fails to capture the audience's interest in the first 60 seconds, no matter how good the presentation becomes, the audience will not listen. It is very important to get off to a fast start with a good **opening.**

Comedians know this better than anyone. If they can make the audience laugh at their opening jokes, the audience will laugh at anything and everything they do or say in the rest of their skit—even if it's not meant to be funny. On the other hand, if the audience doesn't find the first few jokes to be funny, they won't laugh at those that follow, no matter how good they are. What's the message here? Simple: People are very quick to judge, quick to decide whether they like or don't like something. You can see why the opening to your speech is so important.

The Opening

There are two simple but essential building blocks.
- **A Grabber**
- The **WIIFM - W**hat's **I**n **I**t **F**or **M**e (Me = the audience, not the speaker)

Together they should accomplish two things:
- **Grab** the audience's attention by introducing the topic in an interesting fashion.
- Tell the listeners what benefit they will receive from your presentation. This is where you answer their question, **W**hat's **I**n **I**t **F**or **M**e? You give the audience a reason to listen. Let's take a closer look at these two building blocks.

Grabbers

What does every audience have that the speaker wants to grab? If you have read the last few paragraphs, the answer is easy: their attention. How can we do this? By starting with a grabber:

---

a statement, a question, a gesture,
a startling fact, a joke, an anecdote, or a
prop that seizes the audience's attention.

We are all subjected to many grabbers every day. Whether you're watching TV, listening to the radio, driving down the highway past a billboard, or picking up a newspaper or magazine, advertisers are grabbing for your attention. Here are some of their tricks:

Sensory Appeal *Buy this product because it looks or tastes good.* Pardon me, are those Bugle Boy jeans you're wearing.

Snob Appeal *Buy this product because it will make you a little bit better than anybody else* — Guess *and* Oakley *do this.* Pardon me, but do you have any Gray Poupon?

Happy Family *Buy this product because it shows how much you care about your family.* You're in good hands with Allstate.

Celebrity endorsement *Buy this product because You wanna be like Mike.* (Michael Jordan)

Bandwagon *Buy this product because everybody else has it and you don't want to feel left out.*

Humor *Buy this product because the jokes and cartoons make you feel good.* By the way, the Energizer bunny is stillllllll going.

Romance *Buy this product* — *an attractive person like Vanna White uses it.*

Testimonial *Buy this product because an expert recommends it.* Four out of five dentists recommend Colgate.

Just plain folks *Buy this product just because folks like you are satisfied with it.* Ball Park franks.

TV commercials are prepared by teams of scriptwriters who are experts in grabbing your attention. They get paid in proportion to how well they sell the idea. They also have a team of technical advisers to help with spectacular effects. Don't be discouraged and say, "So what am I supposed to do?" Use what they teach us. Here are some types of grabbers you can successfully use in your speeches.

Grab Their Attention with a Question

How many of you would like to earn fifty dollars this weekend?
(A grabber for a speech on how to earn extra money)

Who in the audience would like to earn an A in math this semester?
(This grabber was used in a speech about study skills)

Have you ever wondered what life would be like without clocks?
(Grabber for speech on the history of clocks)

Concentrate for a moment, and ask yourself:
What do I see myself doing five years from now?
(A question grabber for a speech on setting goals)

Do you know who put the E on the top of the Eye Chart and why it's there?
(From a speech about vision and eye tests.)

You can see how these questions would bring forth a response from members of an audience, or at least cause them to stop and think. By doing this, the speaker has grabbed their attention.

Use a Gesture

Gestures, their value and their use, will be covered in chapter 7. In short, gestures include body motions, body language and facial expressions.

Katie, a seventh-grade student, began her speech by dramatically spitting her chewing gum into the teacher's waste basket. She then went on to give a sizzling speech about the pros and cons of the school's new gum policy.

As Kristin walked to the lectern to deliver a speech on gymnastics, she placed her hands on her hips and, to everyone's surprise, threw a complete front flip. Then she calmly approached the lectern, smiled and started to speak.

One sophomore signed the first sentence of her speech in American Sign Language. She invited the audience to guess its meaning: Later she repeated the sentence accompanied by the oral interpretation, "My twin sister is deaf. This is how we talk."

Try an Unusual or Startling Fact

You might start a speech on acupuncture by asking:

> Do you think it's possible that wearing earrings might improve your eyesight? Pirates wore rings in their ears for this very reason. Although scoffed at for centuries, this idea is being reevaluated as part of acupuncture theory.

Let's say your talk is on heart disease and how to prevent it. You might start by saying:

> I'm sure that you'll all agree that one minute is a small unit of time. Yet, I would like you to think about how much your life has changed in the last minute. Probably

not very much. Well, for two of our fellow
Americans it's changed a lot. THEY'RE
DEAD. That's right. During the average
minute of every day—two Americans will die
of a heart attack. Today I'm going to tell you
how you and your loved ones can avoid this
needless tragedy.

A good **grabber** for a speech on automobile safety
might be:

Do you realize that more Americans
have died in automobile accidents than
have died in all the wars ever fought by the
United States?

A student in Arizona used the following **grabber** to
begin her speech on the wonders of her state.

Most people think of Arizona as a desert
state. Believe it or not, it actually snows
more at the Grand Canyon than it does in
Minneapolis, Minnesota.

Tell a Short Story

Use of a short story, true or fiction, is a very effective
means of getting an audience's attention. People love
stories because they build word pictures in their minds.
This enables the listeners to be in an active mental state and
to participate mentally in the presentation. Let's say you are
going to give a talk on the homeless. An effective way to
grab your audience's attention is by telling them about a
homeless person that you know and the struggles they have
gone through. This, of course, would have to be a true
story. Suppose you don't personally know any homeless
people. Then you might create a story.

How many of you slept in a warm bed last night?

Great! Everyone did.

Well, imagine for a moment that instead of sleeping in a nice comfortable bed you had spent the night in a cardboard box in some dark, cold, alley. Instead of a nice warm blanket, you had wrapped yourself in some discarded newspaper.

How many of you ate breakfast this morning?

Well imagine that instead of having cereal, toast, oatmeal, or whatever you chose, you were forced to rummage through a dump site for your breakfast. Hoping… hoping… hoping that someone threw out a few morsels no matter how distasteful, so you could have a meal.

You can see how this little story would form pictures in the minds of the audience getting them to think about what it's really like to be homeless. It will **grab** their attention.

Another example is a story Dr. Snyder has used as a **grabber** in one of his presentations on how to cope with stress.

One day a young dentist (teacher, engineer, etc., depending on the audience) sat at his desk stressed out to the max. He felt like he was going to explode. What to do. "I know," he thought, "I'll go play a round of golf. That will relax me."

Soon there he stood on the number one tee, beautiful blue sky, emerald green grass, golden sunshine, his trusty driver in hand, feeling better already… perfect. Well his first drive wasn't so perfect…. WHAM!! Bang… Zoom… he hooked the ball past the fairway, off a tree (you might say it was a **TREE-mendous shot)** over into the rough on the left.

Darn it! **MORE STRESS.** As he walked out to find his ball, he thought about all the things that had gone wrong that day, and here was one more. Well, when he finally found the ball, he was most pleasantly surprised. Darn if his ball didn't land smack dab on top of a giant ant hill. He knew that even if he were to take a tee out of his pocket and cheat, he couldn't put his ball in a better position.

With a big smile on his face he grabbed his favorite club, his three iron. Man was he excited.

He took a swing.
Whoosh
And another.
Whoosh
Still another, and another…

After he had taken about nine or ten of these practice swings (you see that's what he called them, Heh. Heh.) There were only TWO ants still alive on the entire ant hill. The one ant looked at the other ant with big tears in her eyes and said;

"Agnes, if we're ever going to get out of this mess alive… we had better **GET ON THE BALL!!!"**

Dr. Snyder would then follow-up with this truth:

"And so it is, if we are ever going to get
out of this stress mess alive **WE** had better
get on the ball and do something about it..."

I'm sure you can see already how powerful stories, and the mental pictures that they create, can be. We will get into word pictures in a much greater depth in the chapter on Presentation Skills. Humorous stories are particularly effective as **grabbers.** They are, however, along with jokes, a lot trickier to use. If not used properly, they can backfire. The use of humor will be covered in Chapter 13.

One final thought on using stories as grabbers: Keep the stories as short as possible. You want to grab their attention, but you don't want the story to upstage the body of your speech.

Tell a Joke

Everyone enjoys humor and it can serve to form a bond between the speaker and the audience. Therefore jokes often make good grabbers.

Here are a few examples:

What did one hat say to the other hat?
"You stay here, I'm going on ahead." Well,
today I'm going you tell you how you can
get ahead... ahead in all of your school
subjects.

This was a **grabber** used in a speech on good study habits.

Do you realize today is the anniversary
of the invention of the Venetian blind? Big
deal, you say. Well just think about it. If it
weren't for Venetian blinds... it would be
curtains for all of us.

This **grabber** was used to introduce a speech on inventions.

> I want to tell you about my Uncle Louie.
> He was a curious sort of guy, always tinkering around, always trying to get rich quick.
> Years ago, Louie invented a soft drink. He named it One Up. It didn't sell.
> Louie tried again - Two - Up, but no luck.
> He tried again - Three - Up. Ugh! We hated that one!!
> Then Four - Up, and - Five -Up
> And again - Six - Up
> And then, HA HA, at last
> ...... HE GAVE UP!!!

The speaker could then go on to tell how important it is to be persistent and not give up on your ideas and goals.

Although jokes can make good **grabbers,** the speaker should be very careful in using them. Don't use a joke that doesn't fit in with the speech. It will only confuse your audience and distract from the purpose of your speech. For example:

> Did you hear about the man who crossed carrier pigeons with woodpeckers? Not only does it deliver the message, but it knocks on the door when it gets there. Now I'm going to speak about the value of good nutrition.

A word to the wise on jokes. They can make good **grabbers** but they also have the potential to **bomb.** Avoid off-color (dirty) jokes, those that embarrass or hurt others, or jokes you have to explain. Humorous stories that are real, especially those that actually happened to **you,** are much preferred. No one can say "I've heard that one before" or steal your punchline. Personal experience humor usually gets a bigger laugh anyway. We will talk more about humor later.

Use Props

Props make great grabbers. Briefly, a prop can be defined as any object that aids in your presentation. Posters, books, physical objects, flip charts, the blackboard, a VCR, an overhead projector, and articles of clothing are among the many things that serve as props.

One memorable student, Andrea, demonstrated CPR (cardiopulmonary resuscitation) lifesaving techniques on a lizard. Now, before we really grab your attention, we should point out that it wasn't a real lizard. It was a three-dimensional model. Her **grabber** was a combination story/ prop grabber. She started:

> Imagine a hot, summer day (In Arizona, believe me, it doesn't take much imagina-tion). You step into the backyard for a swim in the pool. You slip your big toe in to check the temperature of the water. AAAHHH. It feels just right.
>
> Suddenly, you see HIM. Oh No! No! No!!! He is floating face down in the pool. You immediately dive into the pool and rescue him in your arms. You guide his limp body over to the side of the pool gently lifting him up onto the deck and you begin CPR...... on your pet lizard.
>
> At that moment, the young speaker reached behind the podium and pulled out the paper lizard. Needless to say, she had everyone's attention and she went on to

teach the current CPR techniques using her
paper pet.

Then there was the eighth-grader who for ten days out
of every summer worked as a circus clown. He carefully
prepared a talk to share his experiences with the class.
When introduced, he entered the classroom dressed in his
complete clown costume. He had successfully grabbed
everyone's attention before he even said a word.

One young speaker began her speech on ideas for
saving the planet by using a balloon as a prop for a grabber.

How many in this room live on the
planet Earth? Good. Almost all of you (This,
of course, got a few laughs and was a **mini-
grabber** on its own). Well, then how many
of you are interested in keeping this planet
alive? Good. If we don't start soon, this is
what will happen...

At this point, she reached under the
podium and pulled out a balloon she had
painted to look like the Earth and a pin.
She stuck the balloon with the pin and...
POP!... she had a super **grabber.**

WIIFM

This is one of the key building blocks of any speech. As
you know, the initials WIIFM stand for *What's In It For
Me*? - with the ME not being the speaker, but the audience.
It's important to let your listeners know that they will
receive benefit from the time they are investing by listening
to your talk.

Here's an example. You love photography and have built a super speech on the topic. Most of your audience might say, SO WHAT? But if you engage the audience first by asking them:

> How many of you have taken photographs of a special family occasion — a birthday, holiday, or graduation — and were disappointed in the results? This has happened to almost everyone. Of course you can't go back and retake pictures of these precious moments — they are lost forever. However, how many of you would like to learn some sure-fire tricks to insure excellent photos in the future? Well, it's your lucky day because I'm going to tell you how to do this.

Do you get the idea?

Sometimes the grabber and WIIFM go hand in hand. For example:

> How many of you are afraid or have been afraid of being assaulted? Well, for good reason. Statistics show that one of every two people in this room will be assaulted sometime in their lives. Since I have a black belt in karate, I thought I might show you how to protect yourself in dangerous situations.

No one wants to listen to a speech, presentation, conversation, or a sales pitch if there is nothing to be learned —no benefit to them. It is very important to try to include everyone in the audience in your WIIFM. In most cases this will be possible.

For example, maybe you want to do your speech on the value of being a Girl Scout. You might state in your WIIFM that males will gain the same benefit from Boy Scouts; therefore, they can see by your talk if Scouting is for them. Or, for instance, you prepare a speech on collecting baseball cards. You realize that most of the girls, and some of the boys, have little or no interest in baseball. You also realize, however, that everyone is interested in money. Can you make money collecting baseball cards? You bet you can. Therefore your WIIFM would include the fact that can earn some dough with this hobby.

Let's return again to the speeches presented in Chapter 4 and examine the **grabber** and the **WIIFM** used by each of the speakers.

TOPIC   PET PEEVES
TITLE   The Pet You Love To Hate
Opening
    Grabber   Fuzzy Puppet
    WIIFM   Learn to recognize and even profit
                 from Pet Peeves.

Now let's review how this part of the speech actually sounded.

The Pet You Love to Hate

(Christi, a fifth-grade girl, stands before the class with a furry hand puppet on her left hand.)

You may not know it, but you all have a pet peeve. No, it's not a cute fuzzy little animal (Caresses the puppet) that you buy in the pet store, but something that really bugs you.

It's like when you put your last dime in a coke machine. (Speaker pantomimes.)

You're absolutely dying of thirst. You push the button and nothing happens.

A solution to that problem might be to put a sign on the coke machine that says, "If I fail to work, please kick me here." (Speaker holds up sign) **(Grabber)**

Many people have profited from the inventions they have made to solve their pet peeves. **(WIIFM)** An example would be the man who got tired of eating stale sandwiches for lunch every single day. He invented the Zip-lock baggy (Speaker shows baggie) and became a millionaire. The Zip-lock baggy has touched many people's lives, and now we don't have to suffer from stale sandwiches any longer.

Now let's check the S-MAP on ventriloquism.

TOPIC	VENTRILOQUISM
TITLE	How to Become a Ventriloquist
Opening	
Grabber	Lambchop Puppet
WIIFM	Fun — Entertain Friends — Occupation

Here's that part of the speech.

(Jessica holds Lambchop, a hand puppet, in her left hand. Lambchop's mouth moves as if speaking.) Wouldn't you like to learn to talk just like me? Well now you can because my friend Jessica is going to teach you to become a ven-trill-o-kissed.

(Jessica speaks) No, no, Baby Lambchop, that's a ventriloquist.

(Baby Lambchops replies) sorrrry.

(Jessica says in a kind tone) That's
O.K.... (Jessica sets the puppet down)
(Grabber)

A ventriloquist is a person who can
make puppets come to life through voices.
Ventriloquism isn't just fun; you can use it to
entertain groups of people or you can even
make it your occupation when you get older.
(WIIFM)

These **openings** are more effective than :

- Today I'm going to tell you about things that
  bother me. *Who cares?*
- My hobby is ventriloquism. *So what!*
- My assignment was to do a speech on
  castles. *Please spare us.*
- I'm going to talk about twins. *Whoop de do.*

We can't emphasize enough how important it is to let
the audience know early in the speech what you are going
to talk about and what you hope they will get from listening
to you. It is critical for you to do this. Don't keep the
audience guessing or they will become confused, lose
interest, or miss your main points entirely.

Titles

You will notice that, at the top of the S-MAP, there is
room for a title. You might mistakenly think you should
therefore come up with your title first. Although this happens on rare occasions, creating a title is usually the last
thing you will do. Finding the right title can be tricky work.
Not all presentations you make will have a title but, if yours
does, you can use it to your tremendous advantage. A title
can serve as a "**grabber**" to get the audience interested
even before you say a single word.

Often, at conventions there are multiple speakers for each time slot. Research has shown that attendees make their choice as to which seminar to attend based upon which title grabbed their attention.

Here are some examples.

1. **Life Is Like a Pizza.** In this speech, the student talked about how involvement in school, family, and outside activities make for a well-rounded lifestyle. He grabbed the attention of the audience by having a fellow student with a delivery hat deliver a pizza to him at the lectern. Inside was a cardboard replica of a pizza with the main topics written on each slice.

2. **Which Button Do I Push?** This title may have the audience thinking of computers, elevators, launching rockets, or a host of other topics. The main thing is that it gets them thinking and involved even before the speech begins. This speech was actually about baby-sitting. The speaker explained that, after several years of baby-sitting, she had found three main ways to get the children to cooperate and exhibit good behavior. She said that one of the three would work on each and every child. (As an additional WIIFM to those in the class didn't baby-sit, she explained up front that these techniques also work well with brothers and sisters, and even on moms and dads.)

3. **Two Words You Hate to Hear Your Teacher Say.** In this student's speech, those two words turned out to be *TEST TOMORROW*. She went on to give some great hints on preparing for tests and how to do well on a them.

Example 4 **Relax to the Max**
(Relaxation Techniques)

Example 5 **Lights of the Future**
(Lasers)

Example 6   **Your Best Friend, Your Worst Enemy**
               (Brothers and Sisters)
Example 7   **Our House is Going to the Dogs**
                (Pets)
Example 8   **Spit it Out**
               (New school policy on chewing gum)
Example 9   **Etslay Alktay Boutay Odescay**
               (Codes)
Example 10   **The Scariest Ride of Your Life**
               (Roller coasters of the world)

❖ Now Try This:

Applying What You Have Learned

Create two **grabbers** for each topic below. Be sure to try a variety of grabbers : Asking a question, giving an interesting or startling fact, using a gesture, a story, a joke, or a prop.

Art	Holidays	Games	School
Food	Music	Discipline	Animals
TV	Books	Hobbies	Travel
People	Places	Current Events	

Then using the same topics build a reason for the audience to listen, a WIIFM.

Now try to create a **grabber** and a **WIIFM** for speeches on the following specific topics.

- How to change the oil in your car.
- The value of physical fitness.
- Saving the bald eagle from becoming extinct.
- Donating blood.

Chapter

6

It Ain't Over Till It's Over

The Close

The third component of a well-constructed speech is the Close. The Close contains three more building blocks we will use at the end of the speech — the **summary,** *another* **grabber,** and the **Call-To-Action (CTA).** Let's examine each one.

Summary

This building block ties your speech together and reminds the audience of what you hope they have learned from your talk. Research has shown that people remember best when they are exposed to material three times. In a well-constructed speech, you are going to tell them what you're going to tell them (opening), then you tell them again using your supporting details (body of the speech), and then you remind them what it is that you have just told them (in the summary building block of the close). This is usually done simply by repeating your main points.

Example 1:

> Today I've told you how you can use Attitude, Backbone, and Commitment as a springboard to a successful life.

Example 2: *From the speech on castles in Chapter 4.*

> So students, in today's lesson we have taken a brief introductory look at these wonderful structures we call castles. We have discussed the history of castles **(A)**, types of castles **(B)**, some of the physical features **(C)**, and strategies used against castles **(D)**.

Example 3: *From the speech about twins in Chapter 4.*

> Today we have covered how twins form **(A)**, some interesting facts about twins **(B)**, and we've looked at what it's actually like to be a twin **(C)**.

Since the Close is the ending of your speech, it is very helpful to use another grabber here to leave the audience with a profound thought, one that will spur them on to action.

Grabber

You probably remember that we covered the grabber in detail when we discussed the opening. You'll also remember that there are a variety of tools you can use to grab the audience's attention (i.e. startling facts, short stories props, etc.). Whereas a grabber in the opening is critical to a successful presentation, a grabber in the close is optional.

It is, however, an excellent way to make a forceful impact on the listener. It will enable you to leave them with a profound thought — one that will spur them on to action.

Examples:

1. Ask not what your country can do for you, but what you can do for your country. *President John F. Kennedy*
2. This is one small step for man, one giant step for mankind. *Neil Armstrong*
3. Every night approximately seven hundred thousand of our fellow Americans sleep in the streets and alleys of our proud nation.

CTA

The final building block in the Close and, for that matter, the entire speech is the CTA. The letters CTA stand for Call To Action. This simply means telling the audience what you want them to do with the information that you have given them. Think of it as a challenge to your listener.

Many speakers, even many professional speakers, fail to use this building block. Yet this gets to the very essence or the purpose of the speech. In sales presentations it is known as "asking for the sale." Many unsuccessful salespeople do a good job of presenting the products and its benefits to the buyer (WIIFM), but they never actually ask for the sale. Successful salespeople live for that moment, the moment when they can move their customer into action.

The importance of the CTA doesn't necessarily mean that it has to be a challenge. It may or may not be.

Examples:

- Now that I've given you all the facts on the school cafeteria policy, I challenge you to sign this petition so that we can get the types of meals and service we deserve.

- Now that I've explained how many dolphins are being needlessly slaughtered by the tuna industry, I challenge you to buy tuna only from those companies that use dolphin-safe nets. (You may list names of those companies here if you desire).
- Practice taking pictures with the techniques that we have just discussed.
- Get up twenty minutes early and exercise each day.
- Now that I've told you how much fun hamsters can be, the next time you consider buying a pet, consider a hamster.
- If you would like to learn more about volcanoes, I recommend that you go to the library and check out *Volcanoes Past and Present* by Ho T. Lava.

Get the idea?

Let's take a look at the S-MAP version of the Close of each of the speeches in Chapter 4.

TOPIC	PET PEEVES
TITLE	The Pet You Love To Hate
Close	
Summary	
Grabber	People who talk too much - TAPE. (Optional)
CTA	Don't get mad — FIND SOLUTION.

Here's the Speech version of the Close:

Here's a solution I thought of for one of my pet peeves, people who talk too much. (Speaker holds roll of tape.)

So, the next time you're really peeved about something, don't get mad. Think of a solution or an invention. Who knows, you might not only help mankind but you may just become the next millionaire.

Notice that the speaker chose not to summarize the main points in this speech.

Another Example

S-MAP version of Close:

TOPIC	Ventriloquism
TITLE	How to Become a Ventriloquist
Close	
Summary	Library — Puppet — Voice — Practice
Grabber	Sadie (Optional)
CTA	Try It.

Speech version of Close:

Here's a quick summary of what I just said. Go to the library and take out a book on ventriloquism. Then get a puppet, create a voice, and practice, practice, practice.

Ventriloquism has a lot of good uses, but I think one of the best is that you get to meet a lot of unusual — but lovable — friends (Jessica shows a small little old lady sock puppet on her hand) like my friend Sadie here.

(Sadie says) That's right Jessica. I'm your frieeeeenddd for life.

(Jessica shrugs and says) See what I mean?

I hope you'll try ventriloquism today.

Example
S-MAP version of Close

TOPIC   Castles
TITLE   Home Sweet Home in the Middle Ages
Close

  Summary   Repeat main ideas A - B - C - D
  Grabber   (Student did not use)
  CTA   Visit Royal Library... visit castles

Speech version of Close

  So my students, in today's lesson we
have taken an introductory look at these
wonderful structures we call castles. We
have discussed the history of castles, types
of castles, some of the physical features,
and strategies used against castles. (SUM-
MARY) I hope you will visit the Royal Library and read a little more on this subject.
You may also plan to visit other castles if
your travels permit. (CTA) You are dismissed for the noon meal, but let's assemble promptly at one o'clock for Sorcery
101.

And One More Example
S - MAP version of Close

TOPIC   Twins
TITLE   Double the Trouble or Twice as Nice
Close

  Summary   Repeat A - B - C - D
  Grabber   Famous Friedman twins, Dear Ann &
                Dear Abby-Kate & Duplicate
  CTA   *Twins* by Jay Ingram - take my advice

Speech version of Close

The subject of twins is not only fascinating, but scientists feel that learning more about twins can be valuable. It just might unlock many of the mysteries about genetics and heredity. If you would like to learn more about twins, there are some excellent sources in our school library. One book I found particularly helpful is *Twins* by Jay Ingram. If you read this book you will learn the identity of the famous Friedman twins, but don't worry, I won't make you wait. As youngsters, they were so much alike and so inseparable that their friends called them Kate and Duplicate. Today they are known worldwide as Ann Landers and Abigail van Buren, Dear Ann and Dear Abby. Each day millions of readers take their advice. I hope you'll take my advice and learn more twins. (CTA)

Earlier in Chapter 3 we emphasized all the reasons why you should not memorize your speech. This still holds true. It is however very important to know the Close to your speech extremely well. Many otherwise good speeches are ruined because the speaker awkwardly stumbles through an unprepared Close, such as :

- That's it.
- I guess I'm done.
- Umm... any questions?

(The speaker should decide if there is to be a question and answer period ahead of time, not on the spur of the moment.)

The impact of a good presentation can be lost by an unprepared or sloppy close.

Remember...

The audience should hear your basic message three times. Tell 'em, tell 'em in detail, tell 'em once more.

❖ Now Try This:

Applying What You Have Learned

Watch at least four commercials on TV. Can you catch the CTA? Which did you like best, the least. Why?

Now develop a Call to Action for these topics:

Art	Holidays	Games	School
Food	Music	Discipline	Animals
TV	Books	Hobbies	Travel
People	Places	Current Events	

Try to develop a CTA for speeches on these topics.

- How to change the oil in your car.
- The value of physical fitness.
- Saving the bald eagle from becoming extinct.
- Donating blood.

Part Three

Making the Presentation

Chapter

7

Six Keys to Unlocking the Audience

Just as important as the speech itself, is the way the speech is presented.

A speech that is poorly prepared but well presented has a greater impact on an audience than a speech that is well prepared but poorly presented.

In this chapter we will present you with six keys. If you follow the guide for constructing your speech and then use these keys in your presentation, you will have a successful presentation every time.

Key 1   Establish Eye Contact

One thing all successful speakers know is that their audience acts as a **mirror.** That's right: Looking at your audience will always be like looking into a mirror. Once, in the middle of a speech, Dr. Snyder slowly put his hand up to his mouth and faked a yawn. What do you think took place in the audience? If you guessed that a lot of the onlookers started to yawn, you are right.

This reaction gave him an idea to put into action. Now after his introduction Dr. Snyder always pauses for a moment and just smiles out into the audience. Not a grin or a laugh, but just a nice friendly smile. What do you think happens? That's right, most of the people in the audience smile back. He has made friends with the audience without even saying a word.

"What does all this have to do with eye contact?" you ask. Good question. If you are paying attention to your audience, your audience will pay attention to you. This is one of the reasons why we don't want you to write your speech word for word and then read it. If you do this, you can't make eye contact. Your attention is on your paper, not the audience.

Now, this doesn't mean that you can't glance down at your **S-MAP** occasionally, or point out something on the board or a chart. Your audience will still be with you. But if you break eye contact with your audience for lengthy periods, just as they have lost your attention, you will lose their attention.

Another advantage of making eye contact is that you increase your impact on the audience (even if there is only one person, like in a conversation). Some studies show that you make up to five times the impact on a listener if you make eye contact.

Dr. Snyder challenges students to try this experiment.

You will ask two friends, your parents, or a brother and sister to do something for you. For example, let's take your parents: Take one or the other, it doesn't matter you choose first. Ask for an increase in your allowance.

To the first, tell all the reasons why this is necessary and how both of you will benefit (WIIFM). But as you present your case, look down at your shoes, avoid eye contact. Suddenly and unexpectedly look up and make eye contact. I guarantee you that the person won't be paying attention to you. They'll be reading the newspaper, watching TV, or just deep in their own thought. They won't be paying attention to you.

Next, go to the other parent. Give the exact presentation, only this time use eye contact. You have a much better chance of being heard and therefore a better chance of achieving your objective.

Making basic eye contact with an audience also gives the speaker more credibility. Often our instincts connect a lack of eye contact with lying. Eye contact also has cultural connotations. In modern American culture, a lack of eye contact is a sign of weakness. You signal that you don't believe in or lack confidence in what you are saying. This is not always true, but this is what is perceived. (Remember: Image is everything).

Interesting enough, in some cultures traditional has taught that making direct eye contact with an elder or a superior shows a lack of respect. In modern times, some of these cultures are backing off from this position as they see how necessary good eye contact is to successful communication.

At first the thought of establishing eye contact is a little frightening, but with a little practice you can master it. Believe it or not, you will even learn to love it once you realize the power behind it. Many of our students refuse to ask someone for a date to a dance or movie on the phone. They want to make eye contact when they pop the question. They know their chances improve considerably because of this simple yet powerful tool.

Key 2   Speak Loudly

We have all felt frustration when fellow classmates get up to make a presentation, a book report, or even just to answer a question — and we can't hear what they are saying. They may have done great research, know their topic well, and have spent ample time practicing their speech. It really should be one of the best. If you can't hear them, however, in actuality it becomes one of the worst. Straining to listen puts pressure on the audience. Most listeners will not tolerate this and will soon tune out.

If your audience is more than just a few listeners, then you will have to speak louder than you usually do when speaking indoors. I always use my outside voice (the voice that I would use if I were outdoors). A good rule of thumb is to pick the person that is farthest away from you and pretend for a moment that he or she is the only person in the room. Speak loudly enough for that person to hear you. If you make sure that your farthest listener is able to hear you then you can be sure that all your listeners are able to hear you. When in doubt, it is always much better to err on the loud side.

It may seem a bit frightening to get up in front of a group and start talking in a loud voice. Surprisingly, though, once you the strength in your own voice, the rest of you will become more confident.

Key 3   Use Gestures

Your gestures (hand, body, and facial) are extremely effective in creating a dynamic presentation and holding the interest of the audience. There are several advantages to using gestures:

They entertain the audience. In a sense, you appear to be acting out your speech. This helps your audience see your speech as well as hear it.

Gestures also help the audience to understand your speech. If you are talking about a birdhouse you built, everyone in the audience might have formed a different mental picture. But if you use your hands to show its height, length, width, or where the windows are, your audience begins to visualize what you are talking about.

Gestures help relax the speaker. Gestures help us to burn off nervous energy. This is one of the reasons that athletes warm up before a game and rock stars usually start out with a song that has them moving around the stage a lot. The more that we lean on the podium or against the blackboard, or the more that we put our hands in our pockets or folded in front of us, the more we block that nervous energy.

One unusual thing about gestures is that we must exaggerate them if they are to seem real to the audience. What seems normal to the beginning speaker seems far too inhibited to the audience. What seems normal to the audience at first usually seems too much to the speaker.

Gestures are actually a part of normal communication. The next time that you're with a few of your friends just talking, observe the others. Watch their hand motions, their facial expressions, and their general body language and posture. You will soon find that we communicate a lot besides the spoken word. Then be aware of your own body language. You will find that we all use gestures. For some reason, the moment that we are in front of a group, we just want to grab something and hold on for dear life. Practice using gestures in rehearsing your speech. Soon you'll do it without thinking, and you'll be giving dynamic presentations.

Key 4   Create Word Pictures

It has been said that *a picture is worth a thousand words*. This is probably a conservative estimate. One of the most powerful tools that a speaker can use is to "paint a picture " in the mind of the audience. Years ago, long before writing was developed, history was passed down by stories. Parents would tell their children stories, who, in turn, would pass the stories on to their children, and so forth. The pictures painted in minds were so vivid that history was passed down quite accurately from generation to generation.

You can paint a picture by means of stories, or sometimes even phrases. Here's an example:

In 1974 Dr. Snyder traveled from his home in Pittsburgh, Pa., to Tucson, Arizona, to take the Arizona State Dental Board Exam. His wife, JoAnn, and their oldest daughter, Sherri, flew with him. Sherri was about six months old at the time.

The return flight back to Pittsburgh took four hours. The plane was no sooner in the air when Sherri, an infant, and tightly strapped in her seat, started to fuss and cry.

A few moments later, they started serving the food. Sherri saw the food slowly coming down the aisle, and not being able to get what she wanted when she wanted it, took her crying up about three notches. By the time the cart stopped in front of Dr. Snyder, she was going bonkers. JoAnn was in the window seat and the stewardess served her first. Sherri was in the middle seat and Dr. Snyder sat on the aisle. They were going to share their meals with her.

The moment Dr. Snyder received his tray, he opened up the entree, which happened to be a meat dish. It was piping hot with steam rising from it. Obviously he couldn't give that to a baby.

His hand shot up to a roll in the upper left corner of the tray. Too hard. No luck there either.

In the upper right corner of the tray was a container of chocolate pudding. He ripped open the bag of plastic silverware and loaded a big heaping spoonful of the brown pudding for Sherri. Her mouth was open, like a baby bird at feeding time. In went the pudding and-wow, relief at last. Or so he thought.

At that moment, Sherri sneezed. HA CHOO!

There were globs of chocolate pudding everywhere. On the roof of the plane, running down the white collars of businessmen, and in the hairdos of women five and six rows away.

The Snyders sank down in their seats so that no one could see them. It's a good thing they didn't have parachutes, because they would have used them. And there were still three hours to go on the flight. Needless to say, it was a very l o n g three hours.

As you read this story you formed some mental pictures as the events were described. You could probably even see yourself on the plane watching the event take place. Had Dr. Snyder been telling the story orally with dramatic gestures, the story would have been even more vivid. Not only gestures make a presentation more interesting, but the audience will remember the information a lot longer.

Here is another example of how word pictures can be created. The following is a true story. Try to visualize the story as you read it. See if the word pictures help you see what was going on inside America West Arena that night.

It was the first win in the new arena, Charles Barkley's first win as a Phoenix Sun, and perhaps the first win in what many believed would be a championship basketball season.

Sir Charles Barkley then swung the basketball around and around and flung it up into the stands. Now, there were nineteen thousand, eight hundred plus people in the stands, and as luck would have it, the ball landed in my outstretched hands.

Immediately people started to say, "Wow, you caught the Barkley Ball! Can I see it? Can I touch it?" People began offering me money for the treasured souvenir. "Fifty dollars... one-hundred... five-hundred... one-thousand dollars."

JoAnn, my wife, our two friends and I drifted with the crowd outside the arena. There, more people shouted, "Look! He caught the Barkley Ball! Can I see it? Can I touch it?" More offers were made.

I was afraid that someone would swipe the ball, so my first instinct was to hail a cab and scramble home. Well, it's true, you can never find a cab when you really need one.

So I quickly tucked the ball under my shirt. What a sight! My wife has carried and delivered five beautiful babies. Now it was my turn.

Well, we finally made it to the parking lot, found our car, and returned home.

Before I entered the house, I stuck my hand inside the door with the ball. I immediately heard screams. "Dad has the ball! Dad has the Barkley Ball!" Our children had seen Charles throw the ball, but didn't know who had caught it.

"Just call me **Sir Kenneth**," I said.

Although stories can be used to create excellent **word pictures**, you don't have to limit yourself to them when it comes to painting pictures in the minds of your audience. Many times a great word picture can be created with a simple phrase or two.

Instead of:

Our national debt is six trillion dollars.

Use:

Our national debt is six trillion dollars. If you laid the dollar bills edge to edge they could circle the earth six times.

Instead of:

The cruise ship we sailed on is 910 feet long.

Use:

Our cruise ship was 910 feet long, or about the length of three football fields.

Instead of :

> My appendix hurt.

Use:

> Pulsating pains shot out of my appendix,
> as though someone had just taken a hot
> poker out of a fire and repeatedly stabbed
> me in the side.

Instead of:

> Being homeless must be tough.

Use:

> Imagine, that instead of sleeping in a
> nice warm bed last night, you had slept in
> some dark, damp cold alley in a cardboard
> box. And perhaps this morning you had a
> healthy breakfast of let's say, rich, thick
> oatmeal, crispy buttered toast, piping hot
> chocolate and freshly squeezed orange
> juice. But what if, instead, you had spent all
> morning rummaging through garbage cans
> and dumpsters, hoping... hoping someone
> had thrown out some bit of food out that you
> could use, no matter how disgusting, to
> satisfy your hunger.

Key 5   Vocal Variety

Nothing will ruin a good speech faster than speaking in
a monotone. Ben Stein has made a successful career using
monotone. Perhaps, you will remember him best as the
social studies teacher in *Ferris Bueller's Day Off*. You have
probably seen him in many commercials since then. He
uses exaggeration to make fun of monotone speakers.

Because we think and hear faster than a speaker speaks,
our tone pattern must vary to be interesting and hold the

attention of the audience. This can be achieved simply by raising and lowering our voice (tone) to emphasize key points. We can also speed up or slow down (rate) to place special emphasis on important points.

The speeches that make the audience the most comfortable are those presented in a conversational tone. Think of the audience as one person — a close friend or a neighbor. In doing so, treat your speech as if it were just a conversation with this person.

In speaking to a rather large audience, you would require the use of a microphone or need to speak a little louder than a conversational tone; however, you can still use the same pacing and words that you would use in a normal one-on-one conversation. Some speakers have a tendency to preach to the audience; this puts the audience in an inferior position. Your best bet is to treat the listeners as equals and make them your friends.

Under Key 3 we mentioned that gestures need to be exaggerated a little bit to be effective. A great way to master vocal variety is to practice exaggerating phrases that run the whole range of emotions.

Example:

I love ice cream.

I hate homework.

If you practice with a partner, when the person uses vocal variety you will be able to see the emotion in their actions and in their faces. Ready for a challenge? Say it as though you really mean it.

I Love Homework.

The proper use of vocal variety keeps you from sounding like a robot in front of your audience. It also keeps your audience from taking a nap in front of you. We will provide more opportunities for practicing vocal variety at the end of the chapter.

The Pause

One aspect of vocal variety that, has a surprising impact is the... *Pause...* If used properly, a pause can build suspense and cause the audience to focus on what you say next. What occurs on a TV show whenever something interesting is about to happen? That's right. They stop for a commercial (a pause) to allow the suspense to build. Watch comedians on TV. They pause right before they deliver a punch line so tension will build and the audience will focus.

Sometimes, after Dr. Snyder is introduced, he will pause and look at the audience with a big smile. If he exaggerates the pause for just a few seconds, members of the audience will begin to wonder... Did he forget his speech? Why doesn't he start? What is he doing? The key to the pause is that he has focused their attention, and only then begins his presentation.

Try the following sentences with and without a pause and see if you don't feel the difference in the impact they would have on the audience.

> (Without): As I slowly opened the box, there,
>   to my surprise, on the bottom was a
>   snake.
> (With): As I slowly opened the box, there, to
>   my surprise, on the bottom, ...
>   (Pause)... was a snake.

> (Without): And, the winner is Bill.
> (With): And, the winner is... (Pause)... Bill.

You can see the impact of the pause. It is also helpful to pause at the end of an interesting or important statement to allow its meaning to sink in before going any further.

In this chapter we have introduced five of the six keys you can use to make any speech, presentation or other form of oral communication come alive.

- Eye contact
- Speak loudly
- Gestures
- Word pictures
- Vocal variety

Key 6   Props

We will cover the use of props — the many types of props and the skill required to know when to use them — in Chapter 8.

The way to master all of the keys is to **use** them. Don't be afraid to risk and experiment. The gain you will realize in becoming an interesting, dynamic speaker will far outweigh the occasional "learning experience" you may have along the way.

Remember...

Coming up with something worthwhile to say is only half the job; saying it in an interesting manner is the other half.

❖ Now Try This:
Applying What You Have Learned

Key 1: Establish Eye contact
Key 2: Speak loudly

Make a conscious effort to use these two keys in all of your oral communications (conversations, talking with parents, answering questions in class, etc.). For one week emphasize these skills. At first it may be a little difficult, but you'll be surprised how easy it is by the end of the week.

Key 3: Gestures

Pantomime (no speaking aloud) the following situations. Remember to exaggerate your gestures.

1. Changing a flat tire
2. Bowling
3. Putting up a tent
4. Building a snowman
5. Changing a baby's diaper
6. Visiting the dentist
7. Giving a haircut
8. Mailing a letter
9. Shopping at the grocery store
10. Washing the car

Key 4: Word pictures

Try this next exercise in front of friends, or if you are alone, in front of a mirror. Using gestures and creating word pictures, tell about;

1. Your scariest moment
2. Something that you have mad
3. Your most embarrassing moment

Key 5: Vocal variety

Pick one or more of the emotions below and think of a time when you have felt that emotion. Then retell the story into a tape recorder paying attention to your vocal variety.

Surprised	Enraged	Happy
Miserable	Lonely	Relieved
Sad	Frightened	
Shocked	Exhausted	

Record these lines with vocal variety;

I hate eating this stuff!

There's no chance, let's give up.

Wow!!!! That's my favorite TV show!

Try combining all of the first five keys in answering these fun questions.

You're Andy or Abigail Ant. Take us on a journey inside of your anthill.

You've seen the movie "Honey I Shrunk the Kids." Shrink yourself and take us on a journey through your backyard.

Imagine that you are a bird flying high above your school. What do you see? How do you feel?

Imagine that you are a drop of blood anywhere in the body. Describe in detail how you feel, what your surroundings look like, what you hear, etc.

You're a basketball at a game. Take us on a journey up and down the court and finish with a slam dunk. Describe what this is like in detail.

Pick one of the finished S-MAPs from your victory list and practice a presentation using the first five keys.

Chapter

8

Using Props

In this chapter we will explore how to use props and visual aids. They can enhance a presentation in the following ways:

- Increase the audience's understanding.
- Help your audience remember what you say.
- Hold your (the) audience's attention.
- Save time for everybody.
- Help you to control your nerves.

Props Increase Audience Understanding

It has been said "a picture is worth a thousand words." If you were to describe in your speech your house, your little sister, or your invention for the school fair (example: a plastic, spring-loaded, automatic electric hamster feeder), everyone in the audience would probably form *some kind* of mental picture based on your description. But if you were to bring your sister, a picture of her, or a picture of your house, or your science project itself as a prop in your presentation, everyone would have a clear idea of exactly what you are talking about.

Help Your Audience to Remember

The more senses we use in an experience (sight, sound, touch, smell, taste), the longer and more vividly we remember it. A speech calls upon your audience's sense of hearing. With props and visual aids you can also stimulate your listeners' sense of sight and possibly their sense of touch. This will help them to remember your talk and to retain more of the material you present.

Hold Your Audience's Attention

We think much faster than we speak. Therefore it is easy for members of an audience to drift into thought ("mind wandering") during the course of a presentation. This is not necessarily a reflection on your speech. We have all sat in front of the TV or read a book and — after a period of time — realized that we have retained virtually nothing. This is because we were in our passive minds. When giving a speech, the key is to get the audience in their active minds. Visual aids and props help the speaker to do this. They encourage the audience to participate in the speech by exploring the props and visual aids that you present.

Props Save You and Your Audience Time

Placing information on graphs and charts makes it much easier and much faster to go over large amounts of material. Pictures and props save time by avoiding lengthy verbal descriptions. And placing information on handouts can save your audience the time it would take them to make notes on the vital information you want them to retain.

Props Help You Control Your Nerves

Visual aids and props give you something to do with your hands. This helps you work off nervous energy. Visual aids also take away the pressure to memorize large amounts of information. Using visual aids is like having your notes right there in front of you. This is a trick or technique used by many professional speakers.

Props and visual aids also help you to relax by shifting the audience's focus from you to your visual aids.

On page 152 you will find a list of some visual aids you might use, with a brief description of the advantages and disadvantages of each. Experiment with as many of these as possible to find out which you are most comfortable with and which ones work in this class and which ones work best for you.

Examples

Jarod started out his speech, *Just A Bunch of Funny-Looking Characters,* facing the audience with an oversized Goofy cap on. The snout was so long that his entire face was in a shadow and the ears drooped down over his shoulders. The audience howled. His prop had the desired effect — it grabbed their attention and set the appropriate mood for his talk.

Lin-Sue, a Korean immigrant, stood before a class of fifth-graders dressed in the traditional Korean schoolgirl regalia. As Lin-Sue told the audience that this is how a

Korean fifth-grader would dress, she deftly led the audience into an account of Korean schools.

Philip held an *I*-shaped piece of metal eight inches high and a quarter inch thick. He asked the students to guess what the object was. He went on to give a terrific speech about railroads. The prop was a cross section of a rail.

A. J. spoke about the intricacies of setting up an aquarium. Before him were displayed all the parts that go into the process. It took him 20 minutes to set up his two display tables, carefully following his planning chart which grouped the props by his Main Ideas on the S-MAP... He then demonstrated how to set up an aquarium.

Erica gave a speech on dreams. Along the way she showed a poster charting the dream cycles that we go through each night. It was easy to see how the cycles become longer and more intense as sleep progresses. It was easy for her to demonstrate that, if we wake up during the dream cycle, we remember the dream. If we wake at the end of the cycle, we cannot remember what we were dreaming.

Meghan displayed a chart on poster board showing the floor plan of the stage.

Pointing to it, she covered the technical terminology of stage directions.

Kevin explained the game of racquetball by using a three-dimensional model of the racquetball court. He also brought a racquet, cans of balls, glove, goggles, and shoes.

Here is a list of some effective props that other students have used:

a grandmother, in person
an Apache wrist bracelet
an audio tape of annoying sounds people make
    while eating
three martial arts weapons
a set of false teeth
Madagascar cockroach, preserved or in a jar
a rap video
a snowboard
an African violet
an autographed picture of Joe Louis
an iguana
potato art
slides of medieval armor
photo of a rock that looks like a buffalo or,
    if turned to the side, a bear

Visual Aids and Props

	Advantages	Disadvantages
Physical Objects, Models, and Props	• Easy to prepare. • Effectively illustrate your message. • Easy to set up.	• Unless a prop is large, you can only use it with a small audience. • Passing the prop around takes attention away from the speaker.
Chalkboard	• Easy to use. • Good for lists and good for writing down responses from the audience.	• Not readily portable-one must be present in the room. • Dusty-requires cleaning after use and members of audience may be allergic to chalk dust. • Can only be used with a small audience. • May not be available to prepare ahead of time. • The "screech" of the chalk may irritate your audience.
Charts and Posters	• Portable. • Inexpensive. • Can be prepared in advance. • Can list audience responses. • Can refer to material already covered.	• Only for small audiences. • Must leave some pages blank so printing does not show through.
Overhead Projector	• Can use with large audiences. • Can use in partially lighted room. • They can be prepared in advance. • Can be used for audience responses. • Making transparencies is relatively inexpensive.	• Depends on availability of projector and screen. • Time involved in preparing transparencies. • Projector must be positioned not to block audience's view.
VCR Tapes	• Can be used with most audiences. • Outstanding images. • Holds the audience's interest. • Creates the perception that speaker is on the cutting edge of technology. • Relatively easy to produce.	• VCR and monitor must be available. • Glare must be controlled and color and screens must be large enough for all to see. • The tape must complement and not upstage your performance. • Time, effort, and cost involved in preparing the video. • Sound bits can be of poor quality. • Multiple monitors or large screen may be needed in large rooms.

Tips For Using Visuals
- Keep them simple.
- Make sure that all of the audience can see them.
- Speaker should thoroughly test equipment and software prior to the presentation.
- Cue tapes and organize overheads beforehand.
- Do not talk to the audience when writing on a chart or board, because you tend to face the board and not the audience.

The Advantages of Handouts
1. They are a take-home reminder of you, your presentation, and the information you provided.
2. You can give lists, statistics, a bibliography, or similar material — information that you want your audience to have, but don't want to spend time one during your presentation.
3. With handouts you can provide photocopies of important material.

Tips for Using Handouts
Make sure that your handouts are neat and easy to understand. Design them as professionally as possible.

Do not pass out material while you are speaking. Members of the audience will start reading the handout and ignore what you are saying. The best time to provide handouts is AFTER the presentation. If the handout contains information that you want the audience to be able to follow as you are presenting it, give them the handout BEFORE you begin.

Remember...

Props and handouts are helpful to both the speaker and the audience.

Chapter

9

The Three E's

This will probably be one of the shortest chapters you will ever read on speaking in public, but it just might be the most important. Most of you have seen the American Express commercials, *Don't leave home without it*. If you have a speech to give, be sure to take along the 3 E's — Never leave home without them.

The First E: Educational

All presentations should be educational. Your listeners should learn *something*. This does not mean that you have to provide them with earth-shattering information. You might teach them something simple, like how to care for a hamster, how to study for a test, or the correct way to change a flat tire — but they should gain new insights.

The Second E: Entertaining

Do not misinterpret this to mean that the speaker must give the audience a "song and dance," but the information you present should be appealing and original. Ask yourself, "What is the most interesting way I can present this material?" It should have your imprint on it. Even serious or sad topics can still be made a lot more interesting by using a little creativity and the six keys covered in Chapter 7.

The Third E: The Big E = Enthusiasm

In most aspects of life, no quality is more valuable than enthusiasm. In public speaking neither knowledge nor preparation can overcome a lack of enthusiasm. Enthusiasm is very contagious. If you are enthusiastic about your subject and your ideas, the audience will "catch" your enthusiasm. I once heard a speaker give a speech on how to change a flat tire. He was so enthusiastic that, by the time he was done, you almost wished your car had a flat tire so you could try it.

If your speech is entertaining, but not educational, that's show biz. Your audience will enjoy your efforts, but will feel cheated at the end. On the other hand, even if you present the best of information but don't make it entertaining, you have a lecture. Anyone who has attended classes knows the result (yawn). But make it educational, entertaining, and add the BIG E - WOW - a winner every time.

Being enthusiastic does not mean that you need to dance and jump all over the stage like Richard Simmons. Although it may work for Richard, it is definitely not for everyone. Show a sincere interest in your subject and your audience will catch it. In the many years that Dr. Snyder has trained students, he has heard speeches about funerals, surviving divorce, the stress of peer pressure, and other very serious subjects. It may seem that enthusiasm has no place in such presentations, but it does. Successful speakers always have an underlying belief in their material, a sincerity that translates into enthusiasm to share with others.

Go back now and think about some of the speeches presented in this book — this time with the three E's in mind.

The Pet You Love to Hate p. 59
How to Become a Ventriloquist p. 6
Home Sweet Home in the Middle
   Ages (castles) p. 79
Double Trouble or Twice as Nice
   (twins) p. 86

Well. There you are, as promised, short but sweet. If it is true that good things come in small packages, let this chapter be a shining example. It has just given you the three most important ingredients for being a successful speaker.

Remember...
   The three E's - *don't leave home without them.*

Chapter
10

The Intangibles

How Do I Control My Nerves?

One day, an unknown singer had the opportunity of a lifetime. Attending a show-case for the record industry's top country and western performers, he was hired for two of the fill-in spots to keep the audience entertained between main acts.

When it was time for his appearance, his nerves got the best of him. He refused to go on stage. Embarrassed, his manager quickly summoned a replacement.

When his next opportunity came, the young singer once again told his manager that he 'just couldn't do it.' The manager came unglued. He reminded the singer of the trouble and embarrassment he had already caused. He vowed that if the singer did not get himself on stage at that very moment, he would never sing as a professional again.

Finding himself between a rock and a hard place, the singer picked up his guitar and sheepishly slid onto the stage. He was terrified. As he began his first song, he could hear his weak voice cracking. Perspiration ran down his forehead and burned his eyes. Yet he could still see his legs shaking uncontrollably. He shuddered to think of the audience's response.

To his utter amazement, they loved him.

The Young Man's Name: Elvis Presley.

Thus was born a legend whose unique style would have a profound effect on the entertainment world for many years to come. We can't all be as lucky as Elvis, but...

When the subject of nerves comes up, there is both good news and bad news. The bad news is that, more than likely, you will be nervous. You aren't alone. Almost all speakers, including professionals, experience uneasiness before speeches. So do athletes, rock stars, actors, and other performers just before their game or performance. The good news is that, not only is this normal, but it's good!!! More news — Nervous energy IS energy. You can use it to your advantage.

When we become nervous, our bodies release a hormone called adrenaline into our bloodstream. Adrenaline causes faster heartbeats, sweaty palms, dry mouths, "butterflies in the stomach," and other symptoms associated with nervousness. Adrenaline also gives us an "energy boost" or "pumps us up" to achieve greater results. If controlled, the nervous energy can increase our awareness and make us more dynamic.

The same phenomenon occurs oftentimes when you are taking a test. As you enter the room where the test will be given, or at the moment when your teacher passes out a test, you feel uneasiness. Even if you've studied and know the material well, you still feel that rush of adrenaline. This is your body's way of telling you that you're ready to do a good job. Like Hans and Franz, you are all pumped up. You probably won't misread questions or make simple mistakes.

In the same way, the nervousness we feel before a speech is your body's way of telling you that you are READY. GO FOR IT!

This nervousness will usually appear just before or during the first few minutes of your speech. After that, you will find that you forget about yourself and focus on your topic. Once you "kick in," your nervousness will greatly decrease. Although you may feel very nervous, even to the point of your knees knocking, or your hands shaking, most people in the audience won't notice. You only appear about one fourth as nervous to the audience as you yourself feel. So realize that your body is providing you with energy… love it and use it.

Here are a few tips to help control nerves:
Do's
- Start your speech with a story, an anecdote, or humor.
- Use props that will take focus off you and allow you to relax.

Remember that nervous energy is energy. You really need this energy to deliver a dynamic speech. (Some professional speakers actually do push-ups or other exercises backstage to create this energy if they feel it is lacking.)

Don'ts
- Take any medication to control your nerves. This will rob you of this special energy, and dull your presentation.
- Use caffeine (coffee or coke) before a speech. This will add to your nervousness and make it harder to harness your natural energy.

Remember: As nervous as you may feel, you only appear about one-fourth as nervous to your audience. Athletes, performers, entertainers, professional speakers crave his energy. Learn to love this natural energy — harness it and, on the day of a speech, don't leave home without it.

How Much Should I Rehearse?

Just as people can't get on a pair of skis for the first time and master them without practice, the same is true for giving a good speech. Professional speakers agree that the three most important ingredients for giving a good speech are The Three P's: *Practice, Practice, Practice.* No professional speaker would address an audience with material that he or she hadn't completely gone over beforehand.

If you want to be a good speaker, you must practice.
Here are some helpful hints:

Mirror, Mirror on the Wall

Rehearsing in front of a mirror is helpful and informative. It enables you to see yourself as the audience will be seeing you. You will also be able to practice gestures or facial expressions. Believe it or not, seeing your reflection in a mirror will simulate being in front of an audience and will make your rehearsal a little more realistic.

Lights! Camera! Action! The Video Recorder

Using a tape recorder (or video camera), record your rehearsal. Then play it back and see if it flows well and achieves the effect that you want it to. Notice also if it makes sense to a listener, is audible, and easily understood. Next, make any necessary improvement then record again.

"Hey Mom, Got a Second?"— Use a Family Member or Friend

If possible give your speech in front of a family member or a friend. This experience will help you get accustomed to speaking in front of a live audience. I hate to admit it, but I've even practiced in front of my dog. A live body is better than nobody.

Close Your Eyes and Visualize

As you practice your speech, pretend that you are actually in the room where you will give your speech. Try to *see* your audience before you. This technique will greatly contribute to your comfort when the time comes for you to give your speech. When Dr. Snyder is speaking out of town, he always asks the hotel or convention center where he will be speaking to send him a floor plan and pictures, if available, of the meeting room. This helps him to visualize what the room will look like as he practices for the engagement. If he is speaking in his hometown of Phoenix, Arizona, he will visit the speaking site far in advance of the speech.

Hear Ye! Hear Ye!—Practice Your Speaker's Voice

As you rehearse, don't just ramble on; practice the tone and voice that you will use in front of the audience. You should be able to feel the enthusiasm in your voice. Practice your pauses and the words or phrases you want to emphasize. Practice projecting your voice to the last row.

Nervousness will tighten the throat and make the voice smaller and higher. Make a conscious effort to speak slowly, and try to project a deep voice to the back row.

Gestures

Practice your gestures. The beginning speaker may have to exaggerate a bit. As you progress and relax, you will be able to rely on your normal body language. Either way, be sure to include gestures in your rehearsals. Don't just sit in a chair or lie on your bed and practice the words. You want your rehearsals to be as real as possible.

Props

Practicing with your props in a rehearsal is a must. For one reason, you will be able to determine ahead of time if something just isn't going to work, or if it will be awkward to perform in front of the audience. You will also be able to pinpoint the proper time within your speech to use the props. As you practice using your props or visual aids, put yourself in the audience's position. Will everyone in the audience be able to see them? Will the audience understand them? Will props distract from the speaker (you)? For example, one high-school student presented a speech on myna birds. As her first main point, she introduced the audience to her pet myna, Gigi. This was fine, but she wanted to hold the bird perched on her arm for the rest of her speech. Unfortunately Gigi wasn't in a cooperative mood and she continuously fluttered and scurried up and down her right arm. Most of the audience was glued to the bird and missed what was actually a pretty good speech.

OOPS — When Things Go Wrong

It doesn't matter how many — or how few — speeches you have given… Things WILL go wrong. The main thing is, … don't panic.

Mistakes in a Speech

In many cases the audience won't even know that you have made a mistake. Remember: You are the only one who really knows your speech. It's not as if you are singing the national anthem or reciting a poem that everyone knows.

If the audience does realize the mistake... so what? You can be sure that there is no one in your audience who has never made a mistake. We all make mistakes. It is part of the learning process. Many people feel that we actually have the potential to learn more from our mistakes than when things run smoothly.

In Chapter 7 we said that the audience is like a mirror. If you don't panic, they won't. If you can shrug off your mistake or even laugh at it, the audience will, too. Never get angry with yourself or anyone else over a mistake. If a mistake occurs, you will have the audience's sympathy. They all know how difficult it is to give a speech and how sometimes things go wrong. If you get angry, it will create a mood of tension and negative energy in the room.

Sometimes when things go wrong, with a smile and a little humor you can turn it into one of the best parts of your speech.

Laugh Lines

Suppose that you accidentally spill water on your notes or something drops on the floor.
    "Hmm...... That's the first time that ever happened..... again.*"

Microphone stops
    (Holding the mic) "Mike! Mike, wake up! There's no sense in both of us dying up here."

You forget a line
    "I've lost my train of thought ...and believe me, it wasn't an express train to begin with."

A prop doesn't work or goes wrong
    "I thought first that I'd show you how *not* to do it."

Here's a *Social Catasterstroke* that actually happened in Tom Murphy's class:

One student, Warren, tried his hand at using props in his now infamous speech: Three Rings Of Fire. In attempting to dem- onstrate the joy of science, he joined three large copper coils to a power source. He then carefully soaked the coils in alcohol.

The entire display was very elaborate and he painstakingly spent his lunch period preparing it, all the while answering many questions from onlookers.

In the meantime Tom had checked the smoke detectors, had the custodian turn off the school fire alarm system for 15 minutes, and brought a filled fire extinguisher to the side of his desk.

As he was introduced, the lights were dimmed, students wiggled to the edges of their seats, and teachers from adjoining classrooms crowded the doorways. This was to be the granddaddy of all grabbers.

To a student drum roll, he lit a match... held it to the center ring... and ... NOTHING HAPPENED.

Well, I shouldn't say nothing happened. Actually, his project blew a fuse and knocked out all of the classroom computers. But the anxiously anticipated "rings of fire" never materialized.

Warren's head bowed, tears filled his eyes, and he was unable to continue.

Several lessons were learned here. First, it was a great effort. Warren had gone above and beyond the call of duty. Second, even though it didn't work, the suspense had grabbed the classes' attention. Third, be careful that your grabber complements your presentation and doesn't up-stage it. Finally, don't cry over spilled milk. If something does not work, simply tell the audience what was supposed to happen and go on with the rest of the speech.

The classroom is your laboratory. The only way you can truly fail is not to try or not to learn from each experience, good or bad.

No matter how much we plan and prepare, things don't always turn out exactly the way we thought they would. Although most people don't realize it, that is what makes life exciting and fun. If we knew exactly how a ball game, an event, or our day was going to turn out, life would soon become pretty boring. The same thing is true of speaking. Every speech and every audience is a little bit the same, and yet, a little bit different. This is what makes it a challenge and also what makes us feel good when we succeed.

A good friend of Dr. Snyder's, also a professional speaker, gave one of his first speeches in a Rotary club. They asked him to speak for thirty minutes. He prepared his speech and rehearsed it many times. Indeed, it was a thirty-minute speech. The big night came and he got up in front of the audience and gave his speech.

When he sat down, he glanced at his watch. He had been up on the stage **six minutes**. He later told Dr. Snyder that he had no idea what he said or what he'd left out. He did, however, learn from this experience. He learned to slow down and relax a little more in front of the audience. Today, he is a very successful, highly paid professional speaker.

Then there was the time…

Dr. Snyder once followed a speaker who used an overhead projector. Dr. Snyder needed one for his presentation, also. As the first speaker showed his next-to-last slide, the bulb burned out. *Social Catasterstroke.* What to do? During intermission, Dr. Snyder tried to find another bulb and even asked for a replacement projector, but no luck. He had to go onstage without a projector. He apologized to the audience for the problem, and then was extra careful to explain his charts and diagrams as he talked.

He learned two things from this mishap: (1) if you depend on a projector, always carry an extra bulb; and (2) try to turn the situation to your advantage.

Often speakers begin a speech with an apology. And it irks the audience to no end.

- I'm sorry, I didn't realize I was supposed to speak today.
- I'm sorry, I have a cold today.
- I'm sorry, I forgot to bring the special props I wanted to show you.

You are going to give a speech whether you are pre-pared, have a cold, forgot your prop, or not. Why even give the audience a hint that they are going to get second best? They don't know you aren't prepared or that you intended to bring a prop. As far as your cold, if it is obvious to the audience. It is better to say, "Even though I have a cold, I feel this subject is so important that I wanted to speak today anyway."

Always make your audience feel they are getting your very best. In your own mind, decide you are going to give them the very best you possibly can under the circum-stances. Win or lose, people respect those who try. So, always give your best effort and learn from the results. The main point I've been trying to make is, even when things go wrong, **have fun**. If you do, then your audience will, too. In a bad situation, **don't panic** and try to turn the problem to your advantage.

Remember…

Nervous energy is **good** energy. Get those butterflies to fly in formation and take advantage of this powerful source.

Good speakers are made, not born. To acquire any skill requires practice. Great oaks from little acorns grow.

Remember Murphy's Law, created by George Nichols in 1949:
If anything can go wrong, it will.
From time to time, things go wrong. Expect it; enjoy it; and go with the flow.

❖ Now Try This:
Applying What You Have Learned

We all experience nervous energy. It keeps us from giving the right answer, getting a date, or creating a good impression. In the next week — whenever you feel uneasy about speaking up — take the risk. Put your nervous energy to use and just do it. In just one week's time you will surprise yourself to see how far you have enlarged your comfort zone.

Always expect the unexpected. ***What if***…
You are giving a speech and you are using a full suitcase of your best gestures. As you spread your hands out wide to make a point, you knock a pitcher of water into the front row all over the audience. What would you do?

You are ready for the first handout, and you suddenly remember they are sitting on the kitchen table. What would you do?

The period before you are to give your speech, you spill spaghetti sauce all over your shirt. What would you do?

You pick up the microphone and feel an electric current running through it. What would you do?

Part Four

Polishing Your Skills

Chapter
11

Introductions

In the case of speeches or reports in class, the teacher usually indicates whose turn it is. That student merely stands up and begins. Often, however, at banquets, graduations, and other ceremonies, a host or master of ceremonies will introduce the speakers. In these situations, as a speaker, you will need an introduction.

Although it is often neglected, this is an extremely important part of a speech. Most professional speakers write their own introductions and go over them with the person who will be doing the introducing. This will cut down tremendously on mispronunciations as well as misinformation, both of which could set a negative atmosphere even before the speech actually begins. A good introduction should include the following things:

1. Introduce the speaker and the speaker's subject.

2. Explain why the speaker is qualified to speak about the particular subject that he or she has chosen.
3. Set the right mood.
4. Inform the audience of the speaker's motive in discussing this topic with them.

Don't leave this important first contact with the audience up to chance or to the person who will meet you only moments before he or she introduces you. The important message here: WRITE YOUR OWN!!!

Below is a typical introduction Dr. Snyder might use for one of his humor (stress management) workshops. It is lengthy, but remember, this introduction was designed for an all-day workshop.

A Sample Introduction
   1. **Introduce the speaker.**
      Ken is a native of Pittsburgh, Pennsylvania. He has lived in Phoenix, Arizona, for 18 years. He loves to play tennis.
   2. **Explain why the speaker is qualified.**
      Ken worked in a soup kitchen for the homeless.
   3. **Set the right mood.**
      Maybe some of you would like to work with Ken in the soup kitchen. Let's listen to his advice on "How Kids Can Help People in Need."
   4. **Inform the audience of the speaker's motive.**
      He wants to encourage each of you to do something special for low income people.

A typical introduction for an in-class presentation might be:

> Jim Jones has been a member of the
> Shadow Mountain track team for four years.
> His main events are the mile and the
> mile relay.
> In his four years at Shadow Mountain,
> he has won six individual awards and
> shared in five team awards.
> Today, he is here to tell us why track
> has at least one event that is right for
> everyone in this room.
> Please help me welcome Jim with his
> presentation… Run to Fun.

This introduction has met the four goals we have established for introductions. Notice how it is much better than the typical unprepared introduction which sounds like this:

> Our next speaker is Jim Johns… ah
> what?… ah that's right it's Jones. Well…
> Jim is going to tell us about track. You're on
> the track team aren't you Jim? I know
> you're in my math class. Well… here's Jim.

Never allow your speech to get off to a poor start because of a poor introduction. Take control of your own destiny and prepare your own.

Remember…

> Don't let a good speech get off to a bad
> start with a poor introduction… **write your
> own.**

❖ Now Try This:
Applying What You Have Learned

Pick a topic that you might use for a speech.
Try writing your own introduction before the speech.
Be sure to:
1. Introduce the subject.
2. Explain why you are qualified to speak on
   this subject.
3. Set the mood.
4. Explain why the subject is important to your
   audience.

Chapter
12

Impromptu Speaking

Impromptu speaking is done on the spur of the moment. In Chapter 3, page 66, we gave a few reasons why this may be necessary. Speaking without preparation seems scary, doesn't it? However, if you think about it, we all speak this way every day. Almost all conversation is impromptu speaking. So are answering questions in class and speaking on the phone. The difference is that, in normal conversation, the spotlight is not on us. When giving an impromptu presentation in front of the whole class, you suddenly feel pressure and your nerves kick into high gear. If this should happen, you want to be a little more organized. Not to worry. There's a super hero here ready to come to your rescue.

Is it a bird?
Is it a plane?
No, it's SuperMAPman.

That's right. By remembering the BASICS of the S-MAP, you can, on the spur of the moment, prepare a presentation. And, by remembering the six presentation skill keys, you can dynamically deliver that presentation.

Example

Teacher: John, would you please stand up and tell the class what you feel are some of the most serious problems facing our nation?

John: (Thinking to himself):

Grabber

WIIFM

A.

B.

C.

CTA

How many in this room feel that our country has problems - I mean serious problems (question - grabber)? Well, I do and I would like to share what I feel are three very serious problems we face (WIIFM).

A. The national debt

B. Pollution

C. AIDS

John could then expand on these, offer some possible solutions, and then challenge the audience to some course of action (CTA) to help solve one or more of its problems.

Now, you might say, "Wow, that John is fast, and he's good, too. I don't know if I could mentally create my S-MAP that fast." In time you will, but at first you don't have to. There is a technique you can use to "buy" a little time while you organize. It is called the verbal stall. This means talking without really answering the question or addressing the subject. Celebrities, sports figures, politicians, and other people who are interviewed often employ this technique to think before they speak.

For example, if John wasn't able to organize his outline quite so quickly, he might have begun:

> Gee, Mr. Cooper. You would like me to explain to the class what I feel are some of the most serious problems facing our nation (repeating the question). You know, that's a very interesting question. There are many problems facing our nation today. Some of these problems affect certain individuals, and some face all of our citizens as a whole. I have often heard my mom and dad dis-cussing some of our nation's problems and, of course, the 6 o'clock news reports con-stantly remind us of them...

Get the idea? Up to this point, John hasn't answered the question at all. He has been using the verbal stall to orga-nize his thoughts. Don't overuse it, however. Don't drone on with meaningless drivel for an extended period of time. The listeners will soon see through your stall and it will work against you. Within reason, however, it can provide the needed time to prepare and organize.

Another way in which the verbal stall helps the im-promptu speaker is by getting him or her started. Once we start speaking, ideas come into our minds a lot quicker than if we wait and "try to think of something." Once the words start to flow, so do the ideas. The silence of saying nothing only makes us more tense and we tend to "freeze".

Another thing that helps with good impromptu speaking (or anything for that matter) is confidence. Confidence is built by doing. Have a friend or parent write some general topics on small sheets of paper. Place them in a hat and, one by one, pull them out and see how well you do. Try to organize your outline mentally, try your verbal stall, and see how long you can speak on each of the subjects.

Some example topics include:

Sports
Right and Wrong
An Example of Beauty
An Historic Moment
A Celebrity
Define What Popular Means
Causes of Teenagers' Stress

You will be surprised that, with a little practice, you will be able to get up and speak, even on topics you feel you don't know much about. You will also be well on your way to being a good, confident, impromptu speaker.

A Final Thought

One of the biggest stumbling blocks most speakers encounter with impromptu situations is that they don't speak in complete sentences. At first glance, this may seem silly, but think about it. Let's look at two answers to the same question:

Teacher: Please tell the class what you think about our school's cafeteria policies.

John: That's an important question to most kids in this class, Mr. Porter. It is an issue that affects all of us. I think the food is too expensive and the portions are too small. Also, I think we should have more of a variety. Another problem is that the lunch hour is too short. Thirty minutes is not

enough time to find a seat, eat and digest
your food, and relax a little before the next
class.

Wow, there goes that John again! Now, let's look at another student's attempt to answer the same question:

Bob: I - uh - think we - uh... Maybe we
need - uh. There are a lot of - you know,
problems. We should - uh - you know - but
then nobody ever - you know. Perhaps
some day we'll - uh - have, you know, warm
food. Some of the problems, you know,
might.... Then again, it's - uh - you know, the
school's fault.

Bob is no exaggeration. We have all heard speakers like that and, unfortunately, too often. Bob may have some really great ideas, but who would actually listen long enough to learn them? At first it will be a challenge but, as you practice, force yourself to speak in complete sentences. It will soon become automatic.

Remember...

Create an S-MAP in your mind and fill in the
blanks.

Start speaking, use the verbal stall if necessary,
but start and the ideas will begin to flow.

❖ Now Try This:
Applying What You Have Learned

1. Pick one of the following topics and try to speak for at least two minutes on that topic. Keep in mind your S-MAP.

Art	Holidays	Games	School
Food	Music	Discipline	Animals
TV	Books	Hobbies	Travel
People	Places	Current Events	

2. See if you can speak for at least one minute on each question.

If you could have any superhuman ability, which one would you choose and why?

If you were to make a time capsule for a future generation, what would you put in it to represent our time and culture?

If you could be any other living creature for a day, which one would you choose and why?

If all of the jobs or occupations paid the same wages, which would you choose and why?

If you could live in any time in the past, present, or future, which one would you choose and why?

Chapter

13

Humor

There is an old saying among professional speakers: "You don't have to use humor in your speech... unless you want to get PAID." Obviously this is an exaggeration, but it shows the importance that even professional speakers place on using humor.

Why Use Humor?

Humor helps the speaker in four distinct ways:

1. Humor Relaxes the Speaker

Most of us are a little nervous when we make a presentation (especially during the first few minutes). Humor helps us to bond with the audience. We feel as though we are one of the group and therefore we can relax. Laughter is actually a tension release. The laughter will drain out your negative energy and refocus it in a positive way.

2. Humor Relaxes the Audience

When the audience laughs, any tension in the room disappears and the audience bonds as one. This is to the speaker's delight because he or she can now speak to the audience as a homogeneous group. Research has shown that whether in a classroom, in front of a TV, or in an audience, people can maintain a high level of concentration for only short periods of time. Humor provides "comic relief." It allows the audience to pause, laugh, relax, inhale a fresh breath of air, and then refocus.

3. Humor Helps Your Audience Retain More

Studies have shown that whether reading, watching TV, or listening to a lecture or speech, people retain more if they are stimulated not only *intellectually,* but *emotionally* as well. Hopefully, our message is "food for thought" and stimulates our audience intellectually. But, if we really want them to remember this information, we must stimulate them emotionally. One way we can do this is by using humor. There is no more powerful, positive emotion than humor (laughter) for accomplishing this purpose. Research has shown that things associated with humor are retained in our memory banks longer.

4. Humor Entertains

Remember the **Three E's** from Chapter 9? There we said how all successful presentations should be **educational, entertaining,** and the speaker should demonstrate **enthusiasm.** Great presentations are both *educational* (we learn something) and *entertaining* (we enjoy). Sprinkle your speech with a little humor and even the what seems to be the dullest topic can become entertaining.

Sources of Humor

There are many sources of humor that we can readily tap to use in our presentations. We will consider six of these sources.

Jokes   Most of us know many jokes, or we can go to the library and find them in joke books. Joke books usually list jokes by topic. The key to using jokes in your presentation is to make sure that they serve a purpose. They should make a point that fits in with your message.

Jokes that don't reinforce your message — those used just for laughs — actually distract from your presentation. They confuse the audience as to the real purpose for telling the joke.

NOT

> Do you know what you get when you cross a carrier pigeon and a woodpecker? ...A bird that not only delivers the message, but knocks on the door. Now that I've gotten your attention, my speech today is on study skills.

BUT

> Have you ever wondered what is the longest word in the English language? Well I'll tell you — it's **SMILE**S — there's a mile between each S. Today I want to tell you three reasons why smiling is so important to all of us.

OR

> Last night I umpired my first Little League baseball game. If you've never been to one, it's like World War II with innings. Well today I want to examine this

concept we call sportsmanship and help
each of us determine whether or not we are
good sports.

You can easily see which jokes fit the speech and which
one doesn't.

Stories   These can be very powerful sources of humor
— providing they help to illustrate part of your message.
Most stories lend themselves to creating great word pictures. Another word for stories is "anecdotes."

Dr. Snyder has used the following story in some of his
stress management workshops.

We had just hired a new dental assistant at my dental office, and it was her first
day on the job. That very afternoon we had
a patient who needed a root canal proce-
dure. (Sounds like fun heh?) The final step
required sealing the opening to the canal
with a putty-like material by means of a hot
instrument. The instrument is heated in the
flame of an alcohol torch. Now an alcohol
torch gives off a very clear flame, and the
new assistant, not realizing this, put the
torch away while it was still burning. She put
the torch in it's proper place ...in the lab
...in the closet ...underneath the toothbrushes ...which were wrapped in cello-
phane.

About fifteen minutes later we were all
running around the office saying to each
other...

"Do you smell smoke?"

"I smell smoke."

"Do you smell smoke?"

Well, my receptionist, the hygienist, myself and the new assistant all met in the lab at the same time. Sure enough trailing out from underneath the cupboard door ...was **SMOKE.** We opened the cupboard door and there sure enough ...was **FIRE.** One of us grabbed the fire extinguisher and immediately doused the fire.

The casualty list included some twenty-six toothbrushes. The tension was so thick you could cut it with a knife. The assistant was the first to speak.

"Dr. Snyder, does this mean I'm going to be fired?"

"Heck no. This is going to make us famous," said the receptionist.

We all looked at her..."Say what ?"

"Sure. We'll call the newspapers, the TV stations, *The Guinness Book of World Records...* Do you realize this is probably the first time ever there was a **BRUSH FIRE IN A DENTAL OFFICE ! ! !**"

We all had a good laugh, the tension was cut, and the safety lesson was learned ...and back to work we went.

Dr. Snyder uses this humorous story to make the point how humor can diffuse stress. (Remember we've already said that it can relax the speaker and the audience.) Always be sure the humor fits your topic. Dr. Snyder uses this fairly long story in the course of an all-day workshop. For a short three to five minute speech, it would be too long. Don't let your humorous story dominate or upstage the rest of your speech and message.

For two more examples of humorous stories, review the "Airplane" story in Chapter 7, page 136, and the "Golf" story in Chapter 5, page 107. You can probably guess that stories that take place in the airplane and the dental office are true, whereas the golf story is made up.

Although both types of humorous stories can work well, it has been my experience that true stories, especially personal ones, work best.

Exaggeration   This technique is used by many professional humorists. We must be careful to exaggerate enough so that our statement will not be accepted as true, but rather as humorous.

Example:

> Let's say you're speaking on the pros and cons of allowances — and you presently receive $5.00 per week. If you exaggerate and say... "My parents give me $20.00 per week!"... some people in the audience might actually believe you. On the other hand, if you were to say..."My parents give me $5000.00 per week!"... you would probably grab the audience's attention and get a few laughs because everyone would know (or should know) that you are exaggerating.

Example:

> We shouldn't curse potholes. They are one of the few things left on the road that are made in the USA.

Personal Humor One of the most powerful forms of humor you can use — and one that fits in best with our speech — is personal humor. Funny things happen to all of us every day. Some of these things may be embarrassing at first, but later — usually after the embarrassment wears off — they make very funny stories. These are unique stories. No one can say, "I've heard that one before," as they often do with a joke. Since the stories are personal, they endear you to your audience by putting you on a personal level with them — by being yourself. Again, be sure that the story relates to your message.

Physical Humor By using exaggerated gestures, we can the audience laughing. There are examples of this on most of TV's sitcoms. Watch a few and see how often the actors and actresses get a laugh during periods where there is actually no dialogue. They do this simply by using physical humor. Facial expressions are also a part of physical humor.

Example:

Let's say that you are upset about the increase in the cost of lunch in the cafeteria. In your speech, you've given your audience several examples. Now you ask them the question, "How do I feel about this?"... but instead of answering the question verbally, you roll your eyes and place your thumb and finger on your nose. You haven't said a word, but your audience is laughing and they get the message — IT STINKS! You have just used physical humor.

Humor Through Props and visual aids can greatly enhance a presentation and add a great deal of humor to your speech. Costumes, funny hats, posters, toys, and stuffed animals, cartoons (held by hand or displayed by an overhead projector) are just a few of the many humorous props that can be used.

Keep This In Mind

Using humor can involve risk — risk that your joke, story, or prop, will fail to get a laugh. However, it is a risk worth taking. In developing your skill as a humorist, you can be sure that sometimes you will not be successful. The important thing is to LEARN from failure …to improve, …and go on. Success is never final and failure is never fatal — unless, of course, you're skydiving.

Humor is an attitude… an attitude that life, school, your job, etc. doesn't cover all kinds of humor. The use of humor in your presentation tells your audience that you are having fun and that you are inviting them to have fun, too. Humor will enhance your speech, but too much humor may distract the audience from your message. Don't try to be a comedian. A sprinkle of humor throughout your speech will help to make it a great presentation — one that your audience will truly enjoy.

Here's a point to watch. Not all humor is appropriate. Ethnic stories, racial jokes, teasing or poking fun at a classmate (without permission) are all forms of inappropriate humor. They really aren't funny. Instead, other emotions come into play and are disguised as humor. In these cases, laughter merely acts as a way of releasing tension and embarrassment. Off-color humor is always inappropriate in front of a typical audience.

Using Humor In Your Presentation

Rule #1
Can Everyone In Your Audience Enjoy the Laugh?
   (No one should feel insulted or hurt!)

Rule #2
When in Doubt, Leave It Out!
   (Don't take chances when it doesn't feel right.)

Remember...

Humor relaxes the audience and the speaker. Humor also entertains. If not used wisely humor can easily backfire, or worse, hurt someone. Humor should complement the presentation and not dominate it.

Chapter

14

Evaluations

A Crucial Step Sharpens Your Skills

It was, for many, the most exciting day of the year in Redwood County. Every year, during the last week of October, lumberjacks and their families would come from miles around and converge on the county fairgrounds for the Lumberjack Jamboree. It was a week filled with fun, festivities, and competition.

The final day was the most exciting, because most of the competition's championships were decided on that day. Especially the most coveted and respected one — Woodcutter of the Year. This distinction was for the lumberjack who cut the most wood from dawn to dusk.

The championship had Tank Patterson pitted against Charlie Meyers. It would be hard to imagine two people with less in common.

Tank was in his early twenties, an outspoken, brash young man. He was large, even by lumberjack standards — hence the nickname Tank. All week long he easily handled the competition as he worked his way to the championship round. Middle-aged Charlie, on the other hand, was short and wiry, a rather unimpressive man. One might mistake him for a college professor rather than a lumberjack. Charlie had not competed all week, but as the returning champ he was allowed to defend his title.

Tank laughed when he saw Charlie. "This will be a waste of your time old man," he said. "I'm going to show you how a real man cuts wood."

Charlie said not a word but just patted his ax.

As dawn broke, the chief judge gave a signal and the competition began. On it went, all day long until at last the sun disappeared behind the wooded hills.

And the winner was… Charlie Meyers.

Tank couldn't believe it. "It's impossible! I'm bigger than you. I'm stronger than you. And I didn't take a break all day. I saw you, Charlie. You took two breaks in the morning, you stopped for lunch, and you took at least three breaks in the afternoon. How did you do it, Charlie? How did you win?"

"You're right, Lad," Charlie replied. "You did see me take quite a few breaks. But what you don't know is that every time I took a break, I sharpened my ax."

In this chapter, we hope to teach you how to "sharpen your ax" and cut a path to improving your speaking skills. This can be done through evaluation. To improve at anything, from time to time we must assess how we are doing. We can then decide what areas need improvement.

Below are some easy but effective methods of evaluation.

Record Your Presentations

I would not suggest video taping until your comfort level in front of an audience is such that you wouldn't be distracted by the camera. Audio taping, however, can be very helpful without providing a distraction. The key here is to let someone else, a friend, or your teacher, run the recorder. This way, you won't have anything but speaking on your mind. Also, make sure that whoever is running the recorder sits close to the front of the room so that you will be heard over any other noises in the room.

When you listen to the tape, don't be negative about your voice (we never sound like ourselves on tape) or your presentation. Listen to the tape like a critic and use it as a learning tool. Make two lists: What did you do well? and What can you do better next time? Also note the audience's reaction to your presentation.

Have a Fellow Student Evaluate You

This can be very helpful. There is, however, a catch. Be sure that the person you pick will give you an honest evaluation. I once asked a professional speaker to evaluate one of my speeches. At the end of my speech he came up to me, warmly shook my hand and said, "Ken, that was the best presentation I have ever heard." Boy, was I on cloud nine! That was only until a few moments later when I overheard him telling another speaker that hers was the "best speech he had ever heard."

We all need *positive* feedback, but to really improve we need honest feedback.

On the other hand, don't choose someone who is too critical. At the end of this chapter is a four-step guide to becoming a good evaluator.

We have found it very helpful when teachers appoint an evaluator for each student. An alternative is to have open discussion by the class for helpful evaluation after each presentation is over.

Teacher Evaluation

Ask your teacher before your presentation if he or she will jot down a few helpful hints to help you improve. If there is a particular part of your speech that you want feedback on, be sure to mention it. After all, your teacher will be the one grading your presentation so he or she should be able to justify your grade.

Effective Evaluation

Through evaluations, written and oral, we not only help fellow students to improve and grow, but we ourselves also learn and grow. The more you speak, the more you will find yourself evaluating the communication skills and presentation skills of others. You may find yourself mentally evaluating speakers, entertainers, politicians and even teachers. This is a valuable practice. By careful observation you will learn techniques and skills that work well, or you can use them yourself. You will also see presentations that are not done so well. You can evaluate what was not done well, what was distracting, and you can eliminate these from your presentations. After all, you don't want to develop bad habits.

As an evaluator, you should not try to point out all of the speaker's faults. Your main goal should be to help the speaker grow and to learn through his or her speaking experience.

Guides to Helpful Evaluations

Be Personal. Remember, even though you have been asked to evaluate, you are only one member of the audience, and your opinion is one of many. Therefore, do not use general statements implying that the whole audience feels the same way you do. Instead, simply tell how the speech affected *you*.

Examples: *I felt... thought... In my opinion...*

Give Positive Feedback. Tell the person what you liked about his or her speech, what was positive about the presentation, what you felt were his or her strengths.

Make Your Criticism Constructive. Don't give negative feedback. Instead tell the speaker how in your opinion he or she could make the speech *even better*. If you feel that an aspect of the speech could be improved upon, give specific suggestions as to how these improvements could be made.

Be Honest. Just because the speaker is your best friend, don't whitewash the evaluation. This means not telling the speaker what he or she could improve upon for fear the person will be mad at you, or that you will hurt his or her feelings. In the long run, you will be doing the speaker a disfavor, and you won't feel good about it either. If you sincerely want to help the speaker to improve and you remember to use constructive criticism as mentioned above, you are on your way to becoming a super evaluator.

Even when you are not assigned to be an evaluator, try to evaluate all speakers you hear (in and out of the classroom). This will help you to improve your own speaking skills.

Remember to take constructive criticism in the right spirit. It is meant to help you improve. Also, try not to work on improving too many areas at one time. This will frustrate you. Pick one or two of the evaluation comments that you feel are valid and work on these. In this way you will be solidly building yourself into a good speaker.

Appendix

On Your Own - Five Surefire Starter Ideas

Speech Project #1
Take A Stand - Solve a Problem

Purpose of This Project:
- For the speaker to learn to put emotion in his or her speech — a very important quality for the successful speaker.
- To gain self-esteem by "taking a stand" on a topic you feel strongly about.

Assignment:

Choose a topic or issue that bothers you, and present your speech so that the audience will be convinced of your sincerity. It may be a political issue, an environmental issue, a school policy, a cause, etc. — any topic or issue that raises emotions within you, and one about which you have deep convictions.

Examples:
1. Gangs - Graffiti
2. Date rape
3. Censorship
4. No pass, No play

Helpful Hints:

Remember to use your S-Map.

The main points might be:
- Something is wrong (needs improvement, etc.)
- Why it is wrong
- How the problem can be corrected.

Although emotion will play a large part in your presentation, you will want to support your convictions with facts, figures, and examples. Be sure to consider other possible viewpoints on your topic and, when possible, explain the fallacy of those positions. Do this without alienating people in the audience who might disagree with you.

TITLE Going Batty

Opening
  Grabber Which mammal flies
  WIIFM Learn why important — myths

Body
  Main Idea **A** Bat Facts
    Detail 1 Nocturnal
    Detail 2 No hair — Blind — Dirty
    Detail 3 Less than 1% — Rabies — Don't
  Main Idea **B** Why important   pick up a sick bat
    Detail 1 Fruit bats — pollinate
    Detail 2 Bat guano
    Detail 3 Eat insects: 1 bat/ 1000 per nite,
  Main Idea **C** How navigate   colony-20,000 eat 1/4 M insects
    Detail 1 Echolocation - 10 high pitches chirps/second
    Detail 2 Use vision also
    Detail 3

Close
  Summary
  Grabber
  CTA Don't squirm - Recognize importance

Sara gave this speech in defense of bats.

Going Batty

Does anyone know what is the only mammal that flies? (**Grabber**) Well, if you guessed the bat, you were right. Bats are very important and today I'm going to tell you why, and I'm going to clear up many of the misconceptions people have about bats. (**WIIFM**)

First of all, bats are nocturnal, which means they sleep during the day and fly during the night. They don't get caught in people's hair, and they aren't blind or dirty. Like other mammals, less than one percent have rabies. Generally, the only way you can get hurt by a bat is if you pick up a sick one and it bites you to protect itself.

Bats are important, especially to farmers, for several reasons. First, fruit bats actually pollinate plants. Bat guano, or bat droppings, are used for fertilizer. We ship this kind of fertilizer to developing countries. Bats also help control insects. In one night, a single bat can eat up to a thousand insects. A colony of twenty thousand bats can eat a quarter of a million pounds of insects in a single night.

Bats navigate by using echolocation. To do this, they chirp ten high pitch chirps a second, and the sound waves from those chirps bounce off any object that might be in their path. This creates a series of echoes that guides the bat around obstacles. Contrary to popular belief, bats are not blind. They use their vision as well as the echo system.

Hopefully, now that I've shared this information about bats, you won't squirm the next time you hear the word bat. I also hope that you now realize how valuable these flying mammals actually are.

Speech Project #2
Win Them Over!
Persuade People to Favor a Bright Idea

Purpose of This Assignment:
- For the speaker to learn how to present a bright idea that is different or controversial.
- To understand that some people in the audience will have different opinions about any subject that you may speak about.

Assignment:

Here's a challenge — one that will test your communication skills. Choose a subject that lends itself to two or more viewpoints. Focus on the least popular of the two and convince the audience that it has some merit. It will be even more challenging if you do not initially agree with the viewpoint that you represent.

Examples:

1. Recycle six-pack holders
2. Students Against Drunk Driving
3. Seatbelts Save Lives
4. Just Say No

Helpful Hints:

Remember to use your S-MAP.

The main points might be:
- Some misconceptions about the popular viewpoint
- Some disadvantages of the popular viewpoint
- Advantages of your viewpoint

TITLE   Learn so you won't burn
_____

Opening   Only YOU can prevent
  Grabber   5/100 fine   4/5 - Home
  WIIFM   Learn fire safety in Home

Body
  Main Idea **A**   Smoke Detector - Demo
    Detail 1   _____
    Detail 2   _____
    Detail 3   _____
  Main Idea **B**   _____
    Detail 1   Floor Plan - show
    Detail 2   _____
    Detail 3   _____
  Main Idea **C**   What to do if fire
    Detail 1   Roll out of bed
    Detail 2   Test Door
    Detail 3   Window — How to Exit
                                  designated area

Close
  Summary   Follow these steps
  Grabber   _____
  CTA   _____

Learn So You Won't Burn

One thing that really helps is a smoke detector. (Melissa holds up a smoke detector.) This one has radioactive material in it that will alert you when there is smoke. Don't worry; it's perfectly safe or I wouldn't be holding it right now. You might want to test these weekly to make sure they work. Some have a button that you press. (Melissa shows a button on hers.) Others require you to light something that smokes to test it. I'm going to test this, and I warn you it makes a pretty loud noise. (She tests the detector, holding it out towards the audience.) As you can see, this one is not going to let you sleep through a fire.

Another good idea is to have a floor plan marking all possible exits from your house. If one exit is blocked, you'll know another way to get out. (Here she shows a floor plan of her house on poster board.) It's important to go over this with the rest of your family so you'll know how to leave your home.

If there is a fire, do you know what to do? Do you just jump out of bed? I wouldn't. If you do you could inhale a lot of soot, smoke and hot ash. This could kill you if you inhale enough of it. Roll out of bed and crawl towards your door. If the door is closed, feel it, because if the door is hot that means that the fire is right outside. If the door is not hot, don't just reach for the doorknob, (she demonstrates) because you might end up with an imprint on your hand like the guy in *Home Alone.* Tap the doorknob with the back of your hand to determine if it's hot (she demonstrates.)

If the door is hot you probably want to go for a window. Don't just jump through the window like superman, because you'll cut yourself or you might be dead like the man in *Ghost,* glass going through your body. (Here Melissa gestures as though there's glass entering her midsection.) Instead, take a chair or something big and then smash it through the window, but stand back so you don't get hit by the flying glass. Then take a sheet and wrap it around you to protect against cuts, and exit the window carefully. Meet your family at a designated meeting spot so they don't send a fireman into the house after someone who's already gotten out.

Please follow these steps and do your part to prevent fire deaths because I don't want to see you dead. (**CTA**)

Helpful Hints:

Make friends with your audience in the opening of your speech. This will tear down barriers and ensure that your audience will listen to you with an open mind. A few ways by which this can be done are:

1. By using humor
2. By recognizing why people hold a popular belief. Admitting that you once held this same belief helps to bond you with your audience.
3. Do not necessarily say that their opinion is "wrong." Let them know that you are here to "provide more facts" for them to consider (and, hopefully, to draw the same conclusion that you have.)
4. Be sure to have some concrete facts and good examples to support your viewpoint.

Be sure to use the six keys:
1. Eye Contact
2. Speak Loudly
3. Gestures (Hand Motions)
4. Word Pictures
5. Vocal Variety
6. Props and Visual Aids

Speech Project # 3
Teach Your Audience
Share Your Knowledge

Purpose of This Project:
- Learn how to organize expert knowledge he or she has into a powerful presentation.
- For the student to learn how to "teach" others.

Assignment:
Present a subject about which you have more knowledge than most of the people in your audience. Topics may include a hobby, a sport you have played, a special skill you have, a country or state you have visited, etc.

Examples:
1. How To Read Music
2. Memorization Techniques
3. Do A Magic Trick
4. How to Pronounce French words
5. How to Trace your Family Tree

TITLE   Smell a Memory . . . Remember a Smell

Opening

Grabber   House / Present

WIIFM   Smells link to memory

Body

Main Idea **A** Facts about Smell

  Detail 1   Average Person — 2000 odors

  Detail 2   Trained expect — up to 10,000

  Detail 3   Linked to emotions - pain/pleasure

Main Idea **B** Odors hard to classify   - demo

  Detail 1   Light spectrum — colors

  Detail 2   Phonetics — Alphabet

  Detail 3

Main Idea **C** Smell benefits Health

  Detail 1   Rotten Meat

  Detail 2   Drs — disease

  Detail 3   Alcoholics

                    Animals communication

Close   Babies / Mothers

Summary

Grabber

CTA   Relate an odor to one of your memories

Topic: **Sense of Smell**

In this speech, Shane, an eighth-grade student, talks about the sense of smell.

Smell a Memory… Remember a Smell

Have you ever walked into a house, and, by the smell, known that you've been there before? Or have you ever received a present, smelled it, and known who gave it to you. **(Grabber)** Helping you understand smell and its strong link to memory is my goal for this morning. **(WIIFM)**

Believe it or not, the average person recognizes up to two thousand odors, and a trained expert can recognize up to ten thousand odors. The sense of smell is considered to be linked to our emotions more than any of our other senses. All smell sensations carry with them an element of pain or pleasure. Most definite smells, people either like or don't like. The same doesn't apply to sight or sound. For example, to ask someone to pick out the more pleasant odor, a rose or a rotten egg, makes perfect sense. To ask someone to pick out the more pleasant shape, a square or a triangle, makes less sense. (Here Shane points to a poster with a rose, a rotten egg, a square and a triangle on it.)

Scientists have not been able to develop an adequate classification system for odors. Nothing that compares with the light spectrum developed for the colors we see, or the phonetic alphabet that we hear. People's ability to recognize an odor they smell is far superior to their ability to name it. Our ability to detect odors can often be beneficial to our health. For example, the human nose is extremely

sensitive to the smell of rotten meat. Some physi-
cians can diagnose certain diseases by their telltale
odor.

Many times odors can bring back memories of
a certain experience in your life. It is very difficult to
break this emotional connection once it has been
established. One benefit of this is that unpleasant
odors have been used to treat alcoholics and help
them to reject drinking. Because of our nose's great
powers, Americans spend millions of dollars each
year to keep from transmitting unpleasant body
odors. (Here Shane sprays under each arm with a
can of deodorant.) Many other cultures have a
much higher tolerance for these odors. Many
animals also use them as a means of communication. Studies have also been done to see if babies
can recognize their mother's odor. The results were
overwhelming. Just about all babies could recognize by smell their mothers over the smell of strang-
ers.

I'm sure you'll agree that the sense of smell is
one of our most fascinating senses. I encourage
you to consider an especially unusual odor and see
if a memory is related. It's helped me to better
understand emotions and experiences I've had in
the past. I hope it will do the same thing for you.

Helpful Hints:

- Use your S-Map.
- Be sure to explain terms or concepts the "non-
  expert" may not understand.
- Think of yourself as a teacher. Your students (audience) should have a greater understanding of your
  subject at the end of your talk.

- Use the Big E - Enthusiasm - to create a "thirst" in your audience for more knowledge on the topic.
- Show the audience how they can benefit (WIIFM) from your presentation, even if they do not want to get as deeply involved in the subject as you have.

Keys

Be sure to use the six keys:

1. Eye Contact
2. Speak Loudly
3. Gestures (Hand Motions)
4. Word Pictures
5. Vocal Variety
6. Props and Visual Aids

Speech Project #4
Shed Some Light
Simplify A Complex Idea

Purpose:

- Learn to use your communication skills to transmit knowledge and aid in audience understanding.
- Learn to break complex ideas into small, easily understood doses.

Assignment:

Take a complex or abstract subject and present it in terms that your audience can easily understand.

Examples

"It Helps to Know Who Your Friends Are!"
You might explain the abstract concept of "friendship" by giving three qualities that

you feel would make a great friend (your A, B, and C in the S - Map) and then give examples of each of the qualities that you have experienced in friends.

"You Gotta Have Heart!"

Here you might explain the complex function of the heart by using easily under-stood concepts (for example, a pump).

"Which Button Do I Push?"

This might be a speech on how we can motivate different people by finding out what motivates them (i.e. competition, praise, fear, etc.).

"Dreams"

In this speech, Stephanie, an eighth-grader, gives the audience information about dreams and how they might be interpreted.

TITLE   Beautiful Dreamer

Opening
  Grabber   Last night's dream — Pets
  WIIFM   Learn more about dreams

Body
  Main Idea **A**   Dream Periods — Rapid Eye Movement (REM)
    Detail 1   4-6 dreams / nite
    Detail 2   Dream periods get longer 5-10 min- 40 min
    Detail 3   Kids 25% more - rt side of brain
  Main Idea **B**   What Dreams Mean
    Detail 1   Falling — Myth — Helpless
    Detail 2   Chased — Afraid to get caught - Dad's car
    Detail 3   Flying — Happy
  Main Idea **C**   _____
    Detail 1   _____
    Detail 2   _____
    Detail 3   _____

Close
  Summary   _____
  Grabber   _____
  CTA   Library — *The Compass In Your Nose*
        and Other Astonishing Facts — Mark
        McCutcheon
        SWEET DREAMS

Stephanie, an eighth-grader, gave this speech on the science of dreams.

Beautiful Dreamer

How many of you can remember dreaming last night? Well, even if you can't, we all did. In fact, we all have several dreams every night, whether we remember them or not. Even animals dream. I'm sure many of you have seen pets twitch (makes a twitching motion with her right hand) and whimper in their sleep. Don't worry, they probably don't have rabies and they're not going into a fit. They're simply dreaming. **(Grabber)** Today I'm going to share with you some of the information we have on dreams and just what some of your dreams might mean.

Every night, you experience periods of very deep sleep. During these periods, your eyes will twitch very rapidly and you may even whimper a little yourself. Perhaps you have seen this occur while watching a sleeping brother or sister, or even one of your parents. This is known as REM, or rapid eye movement. This is when most dreams occur.

Everyone has from four to six dreams every night. Each dream period usually gets a little longer as the night goes on. The first period may be only 5-10 minutes with the last one being 40 minutes. (At this point she displays a graph with four spiked peaks that represent dream periods.) Children spend 25% more time dreaming than adults, and, therefore, are more likely to remember their dreams than adults. In most cases, the only time we re-member our dreams is when we wake during the dream period. Dreams are thought to come from the right side of the brain, and, therefore, those who suffer right brain damage may no longer dream. Sleeping pills and other medications may reduce your dream periods.

Now let's look at what some of our dreams might mean. Have you ever had a dream where you are falling and you woke up just before hitting the ground. Well, there's a myth that if you hit the ground before you wake up that you will die. Relax, it's only a myth. My aunt had that dream and she hit the ground before she woke. She said that she just bounced as though she were on a trampoline. If you are falling, it usually means that you feel helpless and out of control. If you dream you're being chased, it means that you have done some-thing wrong and are afraid of getting caught. For example, last week, I accidentally put a dent in my dad's new car with my bicycle. Neither mom or I mentioned it, and sure enough, that night I dreamt that someone was chasing me. If you have a dream that you're flying, it usually means that you are happy, satisfied, or adventurous.

If you would like to know more about dreams I suggest that you go to the library and take out several books on the subject. The book that I recommend is *The Compass In Your Nose And Other Astonishing Facts About Humans* by Marc McCutcheon... Sweet dreams.

Helpful Hints:
Use your S-Map.

Go to the library and look through some scientific, news, or mechanical magazines to see how they explain complex concepts in terms that are commonly understood.

Try to explain the abstract in terms of "everyday things" your audience has experienced or can relate to.

Keys

Be sure to use the six keys:
1. Eye Contact
2. Speak Loudly
3. Gestures (Hand Motions)
4. Word Pictures
5. Vocal Variety
6. Props and Visual Aids

Speech Project #5
The Personal Touch
Share a Memorable Experience or Person

Purpose:
- To use your communication skills to en-
  lighten the audience.
- Learn to break complex ideas into small,
  easily understood doses.

Assignment:

Recall a memory. It might be the joy of cascading down the Green River in a raft. Or it might be the poignancy of watching a parent trying to overcome a handicap. Here are some examples we've heard lately:

Technology Camp

Megan, a seventh-grader, gave a re-
count of her two summers in Technology
Camp complete with tales of robots, artificial
intelligence, and three-dimensional virtual
memory video laser games.

Miss Lillian

One of the most unusual people in American history, Miss Lillian Carter, was the mother of the President of the United States. She visited with Mark's dad. So Mark interviewed his dad and gave an entertaining speech about the mother of a President who joined the Peace Corps when she was 62. He brought some candid photos of her and a video of the NBC newsclip of the event where they met.

Which Button Do I Push

Melissa discovered that there were basically three ways to motivate the kids she baby-sat — fear, praise, and reward. For example, if she wanted them to clean their rooms. With some children "I'll tell your parents!" got the job done in a jiffy. Others needed to hear, "Of all the children I baby-sit, your room is by far the cleanest." And still others needed the reward of a trip to the park at the end of the task.

This might be a speech on how we can motivate different people by finding out what motivates them (i.e., competition, praise, fear, etc.).

TITLE   Alyssa . . . I Love You

Opening
Grabber   Small World (Play song)

WIIFM   Learning to Cope with Death

Body
Main Idea **A**   About Alyssa

  Detail 1   Died June 23, 1986

  Detail 2   She - 8 Me - 4

  Detail 3   Show Pictures

Main Idea **B**   Alyssa's Disease

  Detail 1   Brain Tumor

  Detail 2   Getting Her to Eat

  Detail 3

Main Idea **C**   Make a Wish

  Detail 1   Show Mickey Ears

  Detail 2

  Detail 3

Close
Summary

Grabber

CTA   Let people know you love them
                 while they are alive

Derek, a sixth-grader, gave the following speech:

Alyssa...I Love You

(During the speech, the song *It's A Small World After All* is softly playing). How many of you here have had to deal with death? **(Grabber)** By that I mean, how many have had a loved one pass away? Well, I have, and today I'm going to share that experience with you. If you've lost a loved one, perhaps my speech will help you cope with that loss. If you are fortunate and have not experienced the death of a close friend or family member, my message is especially for you. **(WIIFM)**

My sister's full name is Alyssa Ann Schaeffer. She died on June 23, 1986. When she died she was only eight years old. I was four. You might think that a four-year-old is too young to know what's going on. Don't underestimate your children or little brothers and sisters. Believe me, I knew what was going on and I understood. (Derek displays a large collage of pictures of Alyssa).

People ask, 'How did your sister die?' Alyssa died of a brain tumor. The odds of her having a brain tumor were one in ten million. At night I wonder and ask myself, "Why? Why did she have to get a brain tumor? Why did she have to be the one?"

The doctors tried radiation to kill the brain tumor but that didn't work. It just stopped growing for awhile and then started again. They then tried surgery to get the tumor out. That didn't work either. So finally they tried some experimental chemo-therapy, which also didn't work.

My sister's brain tumor was located in her skull right behind her eyes and she eventually went blind. When my sister died she was very skinny. Mom, Dad and I tried a lot of games to get my sister to eat. We played the airplane game, you know, the way you do with infants, "open-the-hanger." It rarely worked, Alyssa was too sick to feel like eating.

My sister did a lot of great things for me. She taught me how to talk. She had patience. She showed me how to play games, like checkers and "Old Maid". We played together constantly when she wasn't too sick or tired from her treatments.

My sister was a Make-A-Wish child. Make-A-Wish lets sick children take a trip anywhere they want. She wanted to go to Disneyland and we did, the entire family. (Derek shows the Mickey Mouse ears she got at Disneyland.) My sister's favorite song and ride are *It's A Small World After All*. I really miss Alyssa and I never had a chance to say good-bye. One night she went to bed and the next day she never woke up. My message... no, my plea to you is this... life is so precious, have fun with your sisters and brothers while they're still alive because, when they're gone, you really miss them. **(CTA).** Alyssa, I miss you and I love you.

Helpful Hints:
- Use an S-Map
- Create a list of your unusual experiences.
- Zero in on the one which has the most story potential.
- Try to explain the abstract in terms of "every-day things" your audience has experienced or can relate to.

- Do your best to capture in words what a person was really like, and what he or she meant to you.

Keys

Be sure to use the six keys:

1. Eye Contact
2. Speak Loudly
3. Gestures (Hand Motions)
4. Word Pictures
5. Vocal Variety
6. Props and Visual Aids

S-MAP

TOPIC _____

TITLE _____

Opening

Grabber _____

WIIFM _____

Body

Main Idea **A** _____

    Detail 1   _____

    Detail 2   _____

    Detail 3   _____

Main Idea **B** _____

    Detail 1   _____

    Detail 2   _____

    Detail 3   _____

Main Idea **C** _____

    Detail 1   _____

    Detail 2   _____

    Detail 3   _____

Close

Summary _____

Grabber _____

CTA _____

Success Guides for Students

What! I Have to Give a Speech?
by Thomas Murphy and Kenneth Snyder

Take the "Eak!" out of "Speak!" You can learn to speak in public with confidence. This guide tells you everything you need to know, from how to research your topic to how to use humor effectively. (Ages 12–18.)

BSM, 6 x 9 in., 240 pages, $12.95

Smart Learning: A Study Skills Guide for Teens
by William Christen and Thomas Murphy

Powerful strategies help you learn more, worry less, concentrate better, and get higher grades! Discover how to make the most of study time, take good notes, plan writing projects, prepare for tests, and reach your goals. You'll love the results! (Ages 12–18)

BSL, 6 x 9 in., 111 pages, $10.95